Praise for
When Grandparents B

"Parenting a grandchild is a unique journey full of ups and downs, heart-aches, and blessings. Sharing from his own experience and hard-won wisdom, Rick Johnson's *When Grandparents Become Parents* can be a lifeline of practical information, tools, resources, and encouragement for anyone who is called to travel this path."

> **—Shaunti Feldhahn,** speaker and bestselling author of *For Parents Only*, *The Kindness Challenge*, and *Find Peace*

"I've been waiting for someone to write a book on this growing need for many years. I'm so thrilled that Rick Johnson not only wrote the book but made it so authentic and practical. He is absolutely right when he says grandparents who become parents are total heroes. I meet them every day. This book will affirm their role and come alongside them in a wonderful way."

> **—Jim Burns,** president of HomeWord, author of *Doing Life with Your Adult Children: Keep Your Mouth Shut and the Welcome Mat Out*

"In a flood of emotions, your world has turned upside down. The entire purpose of your life has changed. It's overwhelming. It's illogical. It's beautiful. Thanks, Rick, for giving grieving grandparents a pathway to find new strength, purpose, and joy."

> **—Jay Payleitner,** national speaker and bestselling author of *52 Things Kids Need from a Dad* and *Hooray for Grandparents*

"If you have accepted the daunting task of raising your child's child, you are already a hero. Learn how to navigate 'grandfamily' parenting successfully from one who understands the many and varied challenges and can encourage you on your journey. For the parenting grandparent, this book is a valuable resource!"

> **—Camille Eide,** award-winning author of *The Secret Place*

"Rick Johnson has succeeded yet again in producing a timely resource that will encourage, equip, and enlighten those brave men and women who have willingly taken on the mantle of parenting their grandchildren! Johnson explores the pluses and challenges of re-entering the parenting arena with grace, grit, and hard-earned, real-life wisdom. The author and his courageous wife now parent their deceased son's only child. Readers will discover a familiar friend in Johnson as he candidly shares the struggles they have encountered and how God's amazing grace has met them every time. Read this text for yourself and buy a copy for a friend. It truly is a gift that will keep on giving."

—**Michele Howe,** reviewer, columnist, and author of *Finding Freedom and Joy in Self-Forgetfulness*

"*When Grandparents Become Parents* is a book that has been long overdue in today's world! Thank God for the courage and example of the Johnsons! Rick has penned a power-packed, practical, compassionate, and compelling handbook for grandparents who find themselves as the best caregivers for their grandchildren. Counselors, pastors, and all grandparents should keep several copies on hand as gifts to aid those raising the next generation."

—**Pam and Bill Farrel,** codirectors of Love-Wise and authors of fifty-five books, including bestselling *Men Are Like Waffles, Women Are Like Spaghetti* and *10 Best Decisions Every Parent Can Make*

"We are living in the most turbulent period in modern history. Family dynamics are constantly in flux, and there are many who find themselves navigating uncharted waters. Thankfully, we find lighthouses that illuminate the way and allow us to avoid the dangers that have shipwrecked so many. Rick Johnson is one of those lighthouses, shining the light of truth and reason into the darkness. His message consistently provides hope and practical help. Rick is a beacon to those entrusted with the care of our greatest assets—our families."

—**Tony W. Rorie,** founder and executive director of The Men & Ladies of Honor

"When parents think their child-rearing days are over then get unexpectedly thrust into the role of being a parent to their grandchildren, there are countless challenges and emotional bridges to cross. With genuine transparency, Rick's book acknowledges the feelings every adult in this situation struggles with and becomes the friend they need to assure them that it's going to be okay and that they are not alone. Rick offers hope and encouragement to those who find themselves on this difficult journey and brings to light how raising grandchildren is a high calling, but also a huge blessing."

—Tracie Miles, writing coach and author of the *Living Unbroken* divorce recovery program

When Grandparents Become Parents

When Grandparents
Become Parents
How to Succeed at Raising
Your Children's Children

RICK JOHNSON
Bestselling author of *That's My Son*

SALEM
BOOKS
an imprint of Regnery Publishing
Washington, D.C.

Copyright © 2022 by Rick Johnson
All rights reserved. No part of this publication may be reproduced or transmitted in any form or by any means electronic or mechanical, including photocopy, recording, or any information storage and retrieval system now known or to be invented, without permission in writing from the publisher, except by a reviewer who wishes to quote brief passages in connection with a review written for inclusion in a magazine, newspaper, website, or broadcast.

Scriptures marked with the designation "GW" are taken from God's Word®. © 1995, 2003, 2013, 2014, 2019, 2020 by God's Word to the Nations Mission Society. Used by permission.
Scriptures marked NASB are taken from the (NASB®) New American Standard Bible®, Copyright © 1960, 1971, 1977, 1995, and 2020 by the Lockman Foundation. Used by permission. All rights reserved. www.lockman.org.
Scriptures marked NIV are taken from the Holy Bible, New International Version®, NIV®. Copyright © 1973, 1978, 1984, 2011 by Biblica, Inc. ® Used by permission of Zondervan. All rights reserved worldwide. www.zondervan.com. The "NIV" and "New International Version" are trademarks registered in the United States Patent and Trademark Office by Biblica, Inc.®

Salem Books™ is a trademark of Salem Communications Holding Corporation
Regnery® is a registered trademark of Salem Communications Holding Corporation

ISBN: 978-1-68451-171-6
eISBN: 978-1-68451-207-2

Library of Congress Control Number: 2021946348

Published in the United States by
Salem Books
An Imprint of Regnery Publishing
A Division of Salem Media Group
Washington, D.C.
www.SalemBooks.com

Manufactured in the United States of America

10 9 8 7 6 5 4 3 2 1

Books are available in quantity for promotional or premium use. For information on discounts and terms, please visit our website: www.SalemBooks.com.

Other Books by Rick Johnson

That's My Son

Better Dads, Stronger Sons

How to Talk So Your Husband Will Listen

The Power of a Man

Becoming Your Spouse's Better Half

That's My Teenage Son

That's My Girl

Understanding the Man You Love

A Man in the Making

Romancing Your Better Half

10 Things Great Dads Do

Healthy Parenting

Dedicated to my friend, Diane Markins,
who left us much too soon.

Your vision helped inspire this book.

Contents

Introduction

What's Going On?

Edith was a seventy-two-year-old great-grandmother when her daughter, a single mother, died. With no other family willing to do so, Edith agreed to take custody of her mentally challenged eighteen-year-old-granddaughter. Shortly thereafter, one of Edith's other granddaughters (also a single mom) passed away too—leaving Edith to care for a six-year-old great-granddaughter and a four-year-old great-grandson. Edith and all three kids now live on a small pension accumulated from a lifetime of hard work, supplemented by minor amounts of Social Security death benefits that the children receive. With little to no help or support from other family members, Edith is exhausted and fearful of the future.

Bill and Susan thought their situation would be short-term, but when their son was killed in the line of military duty and their daughter-in-law remarried an abusive man who didn't want kids, they were forced to take in their grandchildren. With another family to raise and college looming for those kids, Bill and Susan's life-long dream of sailing around the Caribbean in retirement has been put on permanent hold.

Mariana is a single grandmother raising her daughter's three children and one of her son's children. Both her son and daughter are addicted to drugs and living on the streets. Due to her lack of citizenship, Mariana is scared of getting involved with the system. Consequently, she has no legal status with her grandchildren and receives no benefits from state or county agencies. She and her grandchildren are living well below the poverty line and barely make ends meet. Thankfully, Mariana is blessed to have a large extended family that helps provide resources and positive role models for her grandchildren.

These are just a few of many similar stories that are repeated every day in our world. While grandparents throughout history have always helped raise their grandchildren, today we are facing an epidemic of people being forced to re-parent their children's families.

If you are reading this book, you probably have a story too. Ours goes like this:

Several years ago, we received the call every parent dreads. My wife and I had been on a date night at a Christian comedy show, having a great time. On our way to the car, we turned our phones back on, only to be met with a sudden barrage of voice messages that created an ominous, foreboding feeling. With trepidation, my wife answered one to learn that our son had tragically and unexpectedly passed away, leaving us to care for his baby girl. It felt like someone had swung a sledgehammer into my stomach. In one instant, our world turned upside down and crashed upon us. As empty nesters, our dreams of retirement and a life of relaxation were suddenly wiped out in a tsunami of grief and new responsibilities.

How do you react to news like this? You hope it's some sort of sick joke or a huge mistake. That day, we joined a club no one wants to belong to—the grieving parents club. I would never minimize someone else's grief, as each experience is different and traumatic in its own right. I have lost both a sibling and a parent, but neither experience was anywhere near as painful as losing my child. Losing a child rips a hole in your soul.

I've learned a lot about grief over the past four years. Did you know that 85 percent of couples who lose a child divorce within five years? So far, we are beating those odds, probably due to the fact that we adopted our granddaughter after the loss of our son. She is also likely the reason I am still walking this earth, as I wanted to die many times over the first two years following his death. Not wanting to leave her the nightmare legacy of losing two daddies probably kept me going.

We took possession of our "li'l bit" when she was sixteen months old and raised her through her pain and grief even as we suffered through our own. The adoption was finalized when she was four. Now, at eight, she is a vibrant, smart, healthy little girl who loves life and is what we politely refer to as "strong-willed."

She has been both a blessing and a bit of a burden, if I'm being honest. As the years have gone by, she has definitely become much more of a blessing, yet the challenges of raising a child at our age continue to be daunting.

However, we are not alone in this adventure. Grandparents raising grandchildren is the fastest-growing type of family unit in the U.S. About thirteen million children live in a home with a grandparent. According to the 2010 U.S. Census, thirteen million children currently are being raised by about 2.7 million grandparents.[1] This has doubled in the past forty years[2] and is expected to grow even larger by the time the newest census is released. For every child in foster care, there are about twenty-five others being raised by their grandparents[3]—saving our society more than $4 billion a year,[4] as well as preventing untold damage in those children's lives. The number of children living in a three-generation household (typically a child, single parent, and grandparent living together) increased about 43 percent between 1996 and 2016.[5]

What has caused this "epidemic" of parents who cannot, or will not, raise their own children? What are the challenges for grandparents? Finally, what are the benefits for grandchildren and grandparents? This book will delve into some answers to those complicated questions, using my own and others' experiences. I've interviewed many of those people for this book but changed their names to protect their privacy.

Typically, the reasons for this phenomenon are "the 'four Ds': divorce, desertion, drugs, and death."[6] Increased rates of drug addictions (especially opioids), abuse or neglect, higher rates of divorce, economic factors, mental illness or physical health issues, military service, death, incarceration, teen and out-of-wedlock pregnancy, and sometimes just plain selfishness are some of the reasons today's adults are leaving it to their parents to raise their children. Even for those who were raised in good homes with proper values, this world can be a tough place, riddled with financial difficulties like college debt, a dearth of good jobs, and little affordable housing. Young people are often hopeless, uninspired, or have downright given up, and children can make these issues even more difficult. None of these are excuses for bad choices or harming or abandoning children, but they may be some possible reasons for doing so.

As grandparents raising grandchildren (commonly known as "grandfamilies"), we face numerous challenges as caregivers. The weight of the challenges that accompany sacrificial love can be a heavy burden. For many, this role is developmentally out of season, unplanned, ambiguous, and undertaken with considerable ambivalence or even apprehension. Additional challenges to raising custodial grandchildren include inadequate support, social stigma, isolation, disrupted leisure and retirement plans, age-related adversities, anger toward the children's parents, and financial strain. Thus, custodial grandparents typically show elevated rates of anxiety, irritability, anger, shame, and guilt—which can create psychological distress that leads to dysfunctional parenting.[7]

This book will give you hope and encouragement, as it provides a plethora of information to help ease your journey of raising a second family later in life. It will outline the challenges, but also the advantages, of grandparents raising grandchildren. For instance, did you know that grandparents who raise grandchildren actually live longer?

We need each other and probably won't get through this on our own. In fact, if you are like me, you need all the help you can get. Here's the good news: this book was designed to give you many nuggets of information to help you along this journey. So hang on and join me for a wild ride through the joys and foibles of being a "grandfamily."

CHAPTER 1

When Your Life Gets Turned Upside Down

No one told me grief felt so much like fear.

—C.S. Lewis

B ob and Mary were enjoying their retirement years by traveling and spending leisure time together. They never thought they'd be parenting young children again, but their daughter got hooked on meth and they had no other choice but to take in her three kids. After years of trying to help her and paying for multiple failed rehabilitation stints, they finally decided they had no choice but to petition the court for permanent custody of their grandchildren. All had different fathers—causing a nightmare of court appearances, Child Protective Services (CPS) visits, and hearings concerning the relinquishment of parental rights before Bob and Mary were finally able to take in their thoroughly wounded grandkids (which by then had increased to four). But the challenges had only just begun.

If you are like me and my wife, your life went from being a happy, contented empty nest to a whirlwind of chaos and drama when we adopted our granddaughter after our son, Frank, passed away. We went from golden sunsets to loud and hectically busy days. Overnight, I went from contemplating my retirement to realizing I'll probably never retire until lunchtime on the day I die.

Or perhaps you've never stopped raising children. Some people live their lives to raise children and are ecstatic about raising their grandchildren. In fact, in certain cultures (even in the U.S.), some women define themselves by being mothers and grandmothers who raise children their entire lives. And to them I say, "God bless you!"

For the rest of us, though, it's important to recognize and even admit some of our less-than-noble emotions in this situation, even if only to ourselves. Personally, I was reluctant, even a bit resentful, to take on the task of raising another child, especially in my late fifties. But Frank's death and his wife's mental illness forced us to take on this herculean task. It was either that or allow our granddaughter to be put into the foster care system—something neither my wife nor I could morally allow, even though our granddaughter's biological mother only allowed us to see her twice, briefly, up until we took custody of her.

When you lose your parents, you're an orphan. When you lose a husband, you're a widow. But when you lose a child (either physically or emotionally), there isn't a name for that. The most difficult thing I've ever had to hear was that my child had died. The hardest thing I've ever done is to live every day since. Know what the saddest sound in the world is? Hearing my wife sobbing in the shower over our late son. One of the biggest challenges we need to deal with, at least initially, is understanding some of our emotions and coming to grips with our grief.

Dealing with Grief

Every grandparent raising a grandchild is experiencing some form of grief. Whether your child has passed away, is in prison, or has succumbed to a life of drug addiction, you have essentially suffered a traumatic loss. You might even grieve for the loss of your golden years, loss of your freedom, or loss of time alone together with your spouse. Grief is the natural result of a loss in life, regardless of what that looks like. That means it's okay to experience these feelings, as long as you deal with them in a healthy manner. Otherwise, grief can turn into depression, anger, bitterness, or resentment—none of which are good emotions to hold on to when raising children.

Usually, we all walk down the corridor of grief on our own. The pastor at Frank's funeral service said something very prophetic: "Dear Lord, help the Johnsons forgive all the stupid things people are going to say to them in the coming weeks and months." So true. One person told me, "I kind of know how you feel. My dog died a couple of weeks ago." *Really? Did you just compare losing your dog to losing my son?*

Many people offered unhelpful or even hurtful platitudes or scripture verses; comments like, "He's in a better place," "It's all part of God's plan," "If you had more faith you wouldn't be in such pain," "God must have needed another angel," and on and on. I understand that people were just trying to be helpful and didn't know what to say, but not only are most of these hurtful, they are unbiblical as well.

We lost many old friends in our grieving process. Perhaps most painful was having people I needed and who I thought were my good friends turn their backs on me—especially peers in ministry. Friends and even family, perhaps because they hurt too much for us or because they didn't know what to say, were strangely silent and have not come around since. Or perhaps because the death of a child fundamentally changes who you are, some of our friends did not want to be around the people we had become. Fair enough. I'm a different person than I was five years ago. In many ways, I miss the man I used to be. But at the same time other people, who we never would have expected such kindness from, have blessed us in amazing ways and helped us get through the most painful time of our lives. We may have lost some old friends, but we also gained many new ones.

My advice is: if you know a grieving parent, talk to them often, even if it's uncomfortable for you. Your discomfort is nothing compared to what they have been through. Mention their child by name often. We love talking about our children in Heaven. We love hearing stories about them. One of the greatest gifts I ever received was when Frank's best friend and his father came over one afternoon. They had been like a second family to my son when he was growing up. We sat around the patio table, had a few beers, and told stories about Frank. We laughed and cried, and it was such a cathartic experience for me. They always remember his birthday by leaving flowers on our porch.

Another friend made a habit of just stopping by out of the blue to take me places like muscle car shows, gun shows, and action movies. Those little things meant so much to me, as they took my mind off my sorrow for a brief time.

Grief has no timeline, and the loss of a child lasts forever. Even years later, your grieving friend is still hurting. Talk to them and lend an ear. You don't even need to say anything—just being there matters.

Stages of Grief

From my experience, grief takes time to work through, typically at least a year and often three to five years (although I doubt we ever really get over it). The death of a loved one has been shown to be one of the most stressful events we can experience. According to Elizabeth Kübler-Ross, author of such famous groundbreaking books as *On Death and Dying* and *On Grief and Grieving*, there are five stages of grief you can expect to go through:[1]

Shock or Denial. Some people do not go through this phase, but others will feel "numb" with no emotions or tears. This stage helps us survive loss. Sometimes there is denial. Shock eventually wears off, and people are able to cry or release their emotions in some other way.

Anger. Boy, do I know this stage. I was angry for several years for a variety of reasons. But anger is a very important part of the healing process. Ross says,

> You may ask, "Where is God in this?" . . . Underneath anger is pain, *your* pain. . . . It is natural to feel deserted and abandoned, but we live in a society that fears anger. . . . Anger is strength and it can be an anchor, giving temporary structure to the nothingness of loss. At first grief feels like being lost at sea: no connection to anything. Then you get angry at someone, maybe a person who didn't attend the funeral, maybe a person who isn't around, maybe a person who is different now that your loved one has died. Suddenly you have a structure—your anger toward them.[2]

This also includes the tendency to respond with irritability and anger towards others. Often there may be feelings of offense or hostility towards family members who do not—or for various reasons cannot—provide the emotional support the bereaved person may have expected from them.

Bargaining, or Preoccupation with the Deceased. Bargaining is where we try to make deals with God, wanting our life to go back to normal and see our loved one restored. In preoccupation, the grieving person thinks about the deceased continually. For example, in this stage a widowed person might continue to feel married for a long period of time. This is normal.

Depression. This is also a stage I am very familiar with. I was depressed for several years after getting over being so angry. Understand that this is not a sign of mental illness but an appropriate response to a great loss. This is not something to be fixed or to "snap out of." Depression is normal for those in grief. Often, grieving people feel total despair, unbearable loneliness, and overwhelming hopelessness. Nothing seems worthwhile. I probably went through at least two years of depression in my journey.

Again, understand that even if your child is still alive, if you have lost them in some way, such as to drug addiction or incarceration, you will be grieving. Recognize your grief and learn how to process it. It's not a process most of us are familiar with. Seeking professional help in no way means you are weak or somehow inferior. You need to be healed and healthy in order to help your grandchildren overcome their loss.

Emotional Release and (Finally) Acceptance. This is where people begin to feel the hurt. If one does not express this emotion, it will manifest itself in other ways, usually physically or emotionally. As an example, for the entire second year after the loss of our son, I was literally sick with one illness or another. None of them were medically explainable. Certainly, they were a symptom of my grief. Men especially may struggle with this stage, as our culture makes men feel uneasy about crying; therefore, they stuff their emotions. Acceptance is not about "feeling okay" with what happened. It is accepting reality and learning to live with it.

Symptoms of Some Physical and Emotional Distress

According to Pathways Home Health and Hospice—an organization offering end-stage health care and bereavement support throughout the San Francisco Bay Area—grief can manifest physically. Some symptoms may include sleeplessness; tightness in the throat; choking or shortness of breath; sighing a lot; an empty, hollow feeling in the pit of the stomach; lack of muscular strength (I literally lost my physical strength for three years after my son died); and digestive troubles or poor appetite.

Other symptoms include:

- A slight sense of unreality
- Feeling emotionally distant from others and believing no one cares or understands
- People appearing shadowy or small
- Feelings of panic, self-destruction, or the desire to run away[3]

These feelings are normal. I am thankful for that, because I experienced all of them.

Guilt. This is a stage not often mentioned by grief counselors but one I feel is important to recognize. There is always some sense of guilt in grief. The bereaved think of the many things they felt they could have or should have done before their loved one died, but didn't. They accuse themselves of negligence. I feel terribly guilty that I wasn't a good enough father

Lily's Story[4]

My husband and I took guardianship of our two-year-old granddaughter, as both her drug-addicted parents were headed to treatment and eventually prison.

Immediately, we noticed her verbal skills regressing. She would fall into this gibberish, followed by a frantic repetition of "mommy daddy, mommy daddy, mommy daddy," over and over again. We just assumed she was missing the parents who had disappeared from her life. It broke my heart.

Her "mommy daddy" rants continued periodically throughout the months that followed, until one morning when I was giving her a bath. She looked up from her water play and said very clearly, "Mommy hit Daddy," then returned to her toys. From that day forward, the gibberish stopped. She had at last found her words to describe the trauma she had witnessed.

or that I didn't do enough to save my son. After all, it's one of a father's main responsibilities to protect his children, even after they become adults.

Your Grandchild's Grief

While we experience grief over the loss of our child, it is nothing compared to what a little child experiences losing their mother *and* their father (and maybe siblings as well). Even more, children typically are not capable of processing that grief and expressing their feelings. Our little one was so sad when we took custody of her. She cried almost continuously when we first got her. Thankfully, my wife had accumulated more than three months of sick leave and paid vacation, so she was able to spend every day of that time nurturing and tending to our hurt little child.

Each city generally has services available to help traumatized children. In Portland, we have an organization called The Dougy Center, whose mission is to provide support in a safe place where children, teens, young adults, and their families grieving a death can share their experiences—all free of charge. I would encourage you to seek professional grief counseling for both yourself and your grandchildren. For smaller children, this might require a professional who is experienced in play therapy, to help them deal with and assimilate these issues and emotions in a productive and healthy manner.

Many people choose not to get help, and then find later on that their grandchildren rebel or act out in anger. Or if you are raising older children, they may already be so damaged that they desperately need counseling. Little people don't know how to process these types of emotions and often act out in tragic or bizarre ways. I'll talk later on about social services that are available specifically for children in these circumstances, and often for the grandparents as well. My point is, don't allow finances to be an obstacle stopping you from getting the help you and your grandchildren need. Children in Oregon (and I suspect other states) that are in foster care or adopted through the state get free health coverage. We haven't had to pay a dime for our granddaughter's medical, dental, vision, or counseling costs since we took custody of her.

You can also get help from a variety of state agencies and nonprofit groups. For instance, in Oregon there is an advocacy group called the Oregon Family Support Network. They provide information and education about youth with mental and behavioral challenges, specifically those with learning disorders.

And don't discount social media. On Facebook, there are several groups dedicated to supporting grandparents raising grandchildren by providing encouragement and resources. I received some great information from a group in Oregon while writing this book called *Ties That Bind: Oregon Grandparents Raising Grandchildren*, which seeks to connect kinship caregivers statewide in order to share their experiences, stories, knowledge, and resources for the sake of mutual support. From what I have discovered, each state has some sort of Facebook support group for grandparents raising grandchildren.

Additionally, The National Family Caregiver Support Program provides help for the growing number of older people who care for children. This program can help those fifty-five and older who are caring for children eighteen years old or younger.[5] I've found very helpful information and support in all these venues.

Other Emotions You Might Experience

You might experience several other emotions when you decide to raise a second family. Some of these might be initial reactions, and some might linger for months or even years. Not surprisingly, women (at least on the surface) seem better prepared to deal with raising their grandchildren than men—probably because they tend to be more in touch with their emotions. Here are a few emotions that I and many folks I've spoken with experienced, and how we dealt with them. They're not all negative, but they all impact you to some degree.

Happiness or Relief. Even if there are a lot of challenges involved, there has to be some amount of happiness, or at least relief, in making sure your grandchildren are safe and well cared for. What a blessing that is in their lives! And as we will discuss in the following chapters, there are some huge blessings in store for you as well. Besides, all challenges in life are easier to handle with a smile and a good attitude.

Resentment or Bitterness. *Why did this happen to me? I already devoted my life to raising my children. Now I'm never going to be able to retire or travel with my spouse.* I suspect that most people have thoughts like these, even if only briefly. They may be natural, but they can be very detrimental to your grandchildren if you do not come to terms with them. Children have good radar systems that allow them to pick up on resentment, bitterness, and of course, hypocrisy in their caregivers.

Trepidation or Anxiety. It's pretty normal to ask ourselves questions like: *Do I have enough money to take care of them? How will this affect my relationship with my spouse? How will I manage this if I don't have a spouse to help? What about my health? Will I stay healthy or even live long enough to raise these kids to adulthood? How can I deal with the various agencies now involved in my life? If there are no agencies involved, how will I ensure I can keep the children and get whatever resources are available to help me raise them?* While these thoughts are

Rhonda's Story[6]

"I'll be right back," I assured my elderly mother. Carefully shutting the car door so as not to wake my two-year-old granddaughter from her sleep in her car seat, I walked briskly toward the store. It was a race against time that my hyperactive grandchild would wake up and find her way across the parking lot before her great-grandmother figured out how to undo her own seatbelt and stop her.

I thrust my three items toward the cashier and tried to catch my breath. The middle-aged woman looked at my purchases and gave me a knowing smile. Still, I felt the need to explain, "The pull-ups are for my granddaughter we recently got guardianship of. The Depends are for my elderly mother. And those are mine," pointing at the feminine products, all the while mumbling to myself that it should be about time for me to be going through menopause.

I grabbed the sack and headed to my car, smiling over the fact that my new life could be summed up with three words—pull-ups, pads, and Depends. Then I spied my happy little granddaughter waving to me from her backseat window, and to my horror saw Great-Grandmother relieving herself alongside the car! Suddenly I felt hot and exhausted. Welcome to my new world.

normal, do not let fear keep you from doing what needs to be done to raise your grandkids in the best way possible.

What Now?

Now you get on with your life as best you can. Even if it's not what you anticipated, you make the best of it. If nothing else, you just keep on keeping on. I once heard a pastor ask a group of men, "Are you man enough to raise the family God gave you instead of the family you always dreamed of?" I think that applies to grandparents as well. Certainly, our life has not turned out the way we always dreamed. But that's the way life is. It's hard, and anyone who thinks it isn't is deluding themselves. But it's our attitude that makes life either happy or unbearable.

After a period of mourning, I woke up and pulled myself up by my bootstraps, to use a well-worn cliché. I decided it was time to make the best of our situation and to lead my new family the best I could. That doesn't mean I didn't make mistakes—and I continue to make them—but I try to admit them, ask for forgiveness, and learn from them. One thing I don't do is beat myself up for my mistakes. Just as I had never been a parent before I had children, I have never been a grandparent parent until now. It's a learning process.

All of us now have to reconcile ourselves to the new world we find ourselves in. It means we now have new roles in life that we may or may not be comfortable with. Regardless, it's going to be a wild and woolly ride.

CHAPTER 2

Our New Roles

Out of suffering have emerged the strongest souls.

—E. H. Chapin

Dave and Judy took custody of their granddaughter when she was two due to her parents' drug addiction. Dave says, "She was ours and we tried to make up for the loss of her parents. We started counseling for her at age three, working on abandonment and detachment issues through play therapy. We went through a neural development plan that required bimonthly travel out of town. Many hours of humorous belly crawls, tactile therapy, and other unusual actions geared to connect both sides of her brain. These neuro-contacts had not developed and were a side effect of in utero addiction.

"Later would come the diagnosis of attention-deficit/hyperactivity disorder (ADHD). That meant learning how an ADHD brain worked. Not only did her brain move fast but so did she! She never crawled. As soon as she could stand, she ran. No need for us to go to the gym, we had enough exercise just trying to keep up with her. Gymnastics, soccer, running, anything and everything to try to use all the energy that Sophia had. I found myself replacing the job I had retired from with a new full-time one of raising a granddaughter. Not exactly what I had planned years before."

Dave concluded, "As we now approach her seventeenth birthday, I look back and see so many happy and interesting memories. They far outnumber the bad ones. Yes, I occasionally wish that things could've been more normal for both her and us. I would like to travel when I want and stay out late with my wife. But those are the little things of life. One day I was thinking, *What if?* while sitting in church. The pastor told us that God is inclined to give us what we need and not necessarily what we want. I decided that was meant for me. So, I think I will just enjoy the ride and carry on. Truth is, I wouldn't trade this experience with my granddaughter for anything. I can't imagine not having her around."[1]

God created within us certain natural roles that we play throughout life. For instance, the parent's role is to teach, nurture, discipline, and develop children into healthy, productive human beings who grow up to lead good lives of their own. A grandparent's natural role is to supplement that of the parent by reinforcing their family values, nurturing the children, and being a sounding board when they need to get perspective from another adult. But most of all, God created grandparents to spoil their grandchildren by loving them unconditionally.

Differences between Grandparents and Parents
(From the Grandchild's Perspective)[2]

Grandmas
- Give me hugs
- Keep feeding me
- Accept me just like I am
- Want me to explain things they don't understand
- Like to smooch
- Say things like, "A few cookies before dinner won't hurt anyone."
- Believe I can grow up to be anything I want to be

Grandpas
- Tell great stories
- Laugh a lot
- Get sicker than dads
- Don't get embarrassed when I do something silly
- Need more naps
- Let me do things others say I'm not old enough to do
- Tell me what I ought to do without it sounding like a lecture
- Know how to say "I love you" with their eyes
- Think that I am the greatest kid in the world

The humorous old saying, "Grandchildren are God's blessings to you for not killing your kids as teenagers" may have a bit more truth to it than we want to admit. There is nothing my wife and I would like better than to spoil the stuffing out of our granddaughter for a few hours (all the while giving her a steady stream of sugary substances) and then turn her back over to her parents. (Knowing we feel that way may be one reason our adult daughter has chosen up to this point not to bless us with grandchildren.)

But in order for children to grow up healthy and happy, they desperately need discipline, structure, and boundaries in their lives. For grandparents who find themselves thrust into the role of parenting their grandchildren, the natural desire of fulfilling your role as a grandparent conflicts with that of being a parent. As my wife and I can attest, this can be very difficult. After all, grandmotherly love is one of the purest forces in the universe. My wife probably struggles even more than I do with having to be a mother rather than a grandma, and the last thing I want to be is a disciplinarian to my little "lovebug" instead of grandpa. But without that discipline, she would grow up to be insubordinate, churlish, willful, and not fulfill her potential—in other words, a brat.

Some of our family members probably already think she is more than a little spoiled. And frankly, we think that's okay. Since she doesn't have another set of grandparents involved in her life, it's a delicate balance that we choose to allow. Plus, we know that she has already suffered more trauma in her short time on Earth than most people do their entire lives. As long as she's a good person, she can be a little spoiled. I have a friend who raised up some pretty darn excellent humans. She said, "It's okay to spoil them as long as they act spoilable."

Regardless of whatever other roles we may fulfill in life, in this situation I believe we are what the Bible refers to as *kinsman-redeemers*. A kinsman-redeemer is a relative (typically a male, but not necessarily) who, according to Old Testament law, had the privilege or responsibility of acting on behalf of a relative who was in trouble, danger, or need. The Hebrew term *go el* (for kinsman-redeemer) designates one who delivers or rescues someone or redeems that person's property. In the Book of Ruth, Boaz acted as a redeemer by marrying Ruth, which took care of both her and her mother-in-law Naomi for the rest of their lives. In the Old Testament, God (or Yahweh) is Israel's redeemer, promising to defend and vindicate the people. He is the rescuer of the weak and needy. In the New Testament, Christ is regarded as a kinsman-redeemer because He helps us in our great need. As a grandparent who has stepped in to rescue your grandchild, you meet all of those qualifications.

Above all else, grandparents provide role models for a child that no one else can. Here are just a few samples of how important they can be. (I'll refer to a child's mother or father throughout the following section. Please know that I am likely talking about you as a grandparent, because you are now fulfilling that role.)

Grandmother and Granddaughter

The greatest characteristic a girl needs in her mother (or another positive female role model) is healthy femininity. In the absence of her mother (or if Mom is an unhealthy role model), the next best example comes in the form of aunts and grandmothers. These women teach her how a woman feels about herself, how a woman loves a man, the respect a woman gives to a man, and what healthy female sexuality looks like. From them, a girl learns how men should treat her, and how to love and live with a man. She also takes her cues on what it means to actually be a woman—how to care for herself and others, how she communicates with others, and how she relates to friends and establishes healthy interpersonal boundaries of all kinds. She learns how a woman manages stress and her emotions, relates to God, and even holds down a job.

I've noticed that my daughter, and now our granddaughter, looks to my wife for guidance, training, and knowledge on many areas of life. Everything from cooking, sewing, and gardening to life stages a female goes through, like puberty and young adulthood. My wife literally saved our granddaughter's life by dedicating many months to feeding and nurturing her, as well as healing her from trauma.

That example goes straight to the heart of femininity. Women care about and value life. They are givers of life. God designed women as more nurturing than men. Without their gifts in this area, a family would never survive, much less thrive.

A woman gives empathy when someone is feeling bad, comfort when they are wounded, and healing when they are in pain. She is more often than not caring, kind, thoughtful, gentle, compassionate, loving, and sensitive. She feels compelled to make sure that children are safe, fed properly, washed, and clean, with all their needs met. Her presence helps children thrive and grow like vigorous stalks of corn in fertile soil. Her nurturing instincts bring vitality to family life. Her healing touch cures everything from scraped knees to bruised egos. Her gentle compassion soothes even the most horrendous betrayal. Women are generally more tenderhearted than men. They are more gentle—caring about people and their feelings. Women tend to be more unconditional in their love, while men are more performance-based in theirs. Women are more likely to be accepting of others and their faults than men are.[3]

Those are just a few of the things young girls learn from older women. But even as girls become young women, grandmothers play an integral part in helping them develop healthy life skills.

Grandmother and Grandson

While fathers (and other positive male role models) are hugely important in a boy's life, mothers and mother figures are also irreplaceable. Much as with girls, they teach boys to understand females and to develop softer emotions. Mothers provide the nurturing, empathy, compassion, and unconditional love boys need to grow into healthy men. Without a female's touch, boys only learn the rough side of masculinity without it being offset by the softer parts.

Boys learn from good female role models what healthy femininity and female sexuality look like, in contrast to what they see in the media. They observe how men and women relate to, respect, and love one another. After all, a mom's job is to civilize a boy. She teaches him the value of serving others, respecting others' differences, healthy communication, good manners, and how to do chores through her example. Without that model, boys struggle to learn what it means to live in harmony with others and can become self-focused. As a friend of mine who lost his mother early in life says, "My dad, my brother, and I all lived like bears. Bears with furniture."

However, boys raised with *only* female role models in their lives face a plethora of problems, and those only raised by their grandmothers tend to have significantly more difficulties than girls. Manhood and healthy masculinity are learned behaviors, and boys learn to become men by observing other men. Without that model they suffer; without proper discipline and boundaries, they can become reckless and make poor choices in life. Boys who are rescued too often by women develop some bad habits—usually for a lifetime.

Kids from single-parent homes are more vulnerable to being preyed upon in a variety of ways (such as physical abuse or sexual assault), suffer from poverty, and are much more likely to develop substance-abuse issues, engage in sexual promiscuity, or get involved in criminal activities. Children from single-parent homes are far more likely to score significantly more poorly on every measurable educational outcome than children from intact families.[4]

Very often, boys who only get to observe a feminine perspective on responding to life learn to expect to be "rescued" by Mom (or another female) and are frequently reluctant to try new things. When they do, they tend to quit easily.

These boys also are often angry. Sometimes their anger is externalized and apparent in social and educational venues, and other times it is internalized into passive-aggressive behavior. Frankly, they have a right to be angry—they have been deprived of their God-given right to a man teaching them how to make their way in this big, harsh world. They do not have a father to teach them, protect them, and empathize with their struggles. Frequently, though, this anger is used to cover other emotions such as fear, humiliation, anxiety, vulnerability, or even pain. Unless boys are taught to recognize this, they are doomed to believe they can solve any problem in life using anger and other unhealthy coping mechanisms.[5]

If you are a grandmother raising a grandson on your own, I want to encourage you to recognize his need for a positive male role model and find a healthy way to provide one.

Grandfather and Grandson
Why do we sometimes see people who had horrible childhoods turn out to be wonderful, productive citizens? Conversely, we also see kids from great homes who turn out to be criminals, or at the very least make poor decisions throughout life. I don't know the answer to those questions, but I do know that boys who do not have positive male role models face significant disadvantages as they grow up and try to become men.

In nature, young mammals must be taught by their parent(s) and other mentors the skills necessary to survive. Adults teach those skills through modeling behaviors over and over again until the young have adopted them. Without that training, they perish. A young bear, elk, or cougar dies quickly without a parent around. Our young people are the same way. Without proper training on how to succeed in life, they make choices that cause them and their offspring to perish rather than thrive.

I am convinced that the greatest, most effective way we can help other people is through mentoring. Being mentored or guided by positive role models is also the best way that people learn, especially boys. Males are extremely visual, so the need to actually see an example is imperative to our learning and developmental processes. All males need older males to guide them through various stages of life.

As men, we are frequently called upon to use our long-range vision, discernment, and experience to protect those we love without them even knowing it. It is how we teach and guide those under our care. And receiving guidance about life from a father is very often how boys receive love.

Boys need to start getting hardened for life by their fathers and other older men. Life is tough. Boys who enter life "soft" find themselves at a big disadvantage in trying to succeed and lead their families.

Men have been given tremendous power to impact people's lives—for good or ill—by the things we do or don't do. Most men I know either don't recognize or don't understand this power. When I speak at conferences on the tremendous power we have, men are always surprised and somewhat shocked. I suspect it is because our culture never tells them of this life-changing energy God has bestowed upon us. In fact, it is just the opposite: our society (movies, television, commercials, etc.) seems to go out of its way to destroy and belittle masculinity.

Every boy needs to hear his father (or grandfather) say two things: *I love you* and *I'm proud of you*. He also needs to be taught by a man how to face life, and how a man thinks, acts, and solves problems. Without that blessing, a boy/man will search for it and try to earn it throughout his lifetime, becoming frustrated when he doesn't receive it. God granted men and fathers a magnificent power to positively impact their own wives and children, and also other women and children. It is a power that a man can choose to use, not use, or abuse. Whatever he chooses, with great power comes great responsibility.

Grandfather and Granddaughter

Fathers and important father figures (such as grandfathers) have a tremendous ability to influence the lives of their daughters, either positively or negatively. How a father (or father figure) treats his daughter will shape how she views herself and how she expects other men to treat her for the rest of her life. A father sets a huge example for his daughter regarding the qualities she looks for in a man and the standards she maintains in her relationships. He even determines how a girl feels about herself: if a father shows his daughter love, respect, and appreciation for who she is, she will believe she deserves this as a woman, no matter what anyone else thinks.[6]

As male role models, we even impact the intellectual, emotional, and physical development of the girls in our lives. Toddlers with father attachments have better problem-solving skills. Girls with close father relationships are more academically successful. As a girl gets older, father-connectedness is the number one factor in delaying and preventing her from engaging in premarital sex and drug and alcohol abuse.[7] Girls with involved fathers are more assertive and have higher self-esteem.[8] Also, girls with involved fathers have higher quantitative and verbal skills and higher intellectual functioning.[9] (And you just thought you were Grandpa.)

Our spoken and written words contain great power as well. Because a daughter so yearns to secure the love of her father, she believes what her father believes about her. If he calls her stupid or incompetent, she will believe that about herself. But if he calls her intelligent, beautiful, competent, and accomplished, then she will believe that to be true.[10] I was listening to a radio show once on which a woman talked about a paper-coated clothes hanger that was her most cherished possession. Her father had written "I love you" on it when she was a little girl. She carried it with her all through college and into her marriage. Now as an elderly woman, she still cherishes it. Never underestimate the power of the phrases "I love you" or "I'm proud of you" and especially with girls, "You are so beautiful and intelligent!" I've met too many mature people who said their only regret in life was that they never heard their father say one of those things to them.

What's In a Name?

One interesting sidenote to consider is how your grandchildren should address you. I suspect their age when they move in with you will make a big difference in what they call you. Since our granddaughter was virtually a baby (just sixteen months old) when we took custody of her, she recognizes us as her parents (or perhaps the need and desire to have someone you can call your parents is so strong that she is willing to accept us as a substitute). She was four years old when the adoption was finalized, so she is well aware that we are her grandparents, not her biological parents. Initially "E" (our nickname for her) called me "Poppy." That didn't last very long before she started calling me "Dad" (never "Daddy"). Now that's the only thing she calls me. She started out calling our son "Daddy," but as she grew, she began referring to him as her "birth dad" or "Daddy Frank." Now, she just refers to him as "Frank" or "Frankie," despite the fact that I always refer to our late son as her daddy.

What I find fascinating is that she calls my wife both "Grandma" and "Mom." I suspect it is subconscious, but I've observed that when she wants food or any other type of nurturing, she frequently calls her "Grandma." Most other times she calls her "Mom." (We get interesting looks from people in public when she calls me "Dad" and my wife "Grandma" in the same sentence.) I've spoken with some grandmothers who were uncomfortable having their grandchildren call them "Mom." They somehow felt it was disloyal to the biological mother. My thought is that all young children need a mommy. Mothers nurture and love children. If you fulfill that role, for all intents and purposes you *are* that child's mother. If it makes the child feel more loved and secure to call you "Mom" or "Dad," I say suffer whatever discomfort you might feel for his or her benefit.

I don't think it really matters what your grandchild calls you, as long as it isn't disrespectful. Whether they call women Nana, Grammy, Mimi, Nanny, Mamaw, or Gram, or men get called Papa, Granddad, Pop-Pop, Poppy, Papaw, or Pappy, it's all good. Or little ones might even call you some completely made-up name. Regardless, they are expressions of love.

I always wanted our granddaughter to decide what to call us—whatever she was comfortable with. I never even suggested any names. The trauma of leaving one family and melding into another is bad enough without worrying about titles, in my opinion. Other people appear to be more confused about what to call us than she is. She always refers to us as her parents, but it's kind of fun to watch other people stammer and stutter over what to call us. In public, I tend to either just call E "my daughter" or my "daughter/granddaughter," which is a bit more cumbersome.

CHAPTER 3

Challenges of Raising Children Later in Life

Don't worry that children never listen to you; worry that they are always watching you.

—Robert Fulghum

Parenting can be a thankless job. As a grandparent raising your grandchildren, it's even more strenuous. Grandparents raising grandchildren face staggering challenges. Much of the time it can feel like a full-time job with no vacation. Some of the challenges grandparents cite include exhaustion or lack of energy, feeling emotionally and mentally overwhelmed, lack of resources or finances, feeling hopeless and isolated, trying to navigate the "system," not being able to be a "grandparent," and receiving no help with childcare. They often have less time for themselves and less time to spend with their partners and friends. This loss of social connections can be stressful and can contribute to depression and feelings of guilt, shame, anger, loss, and grief. What do you do when you feel like your first round of parenting didn't turn out like you hoped, and you're dealing with a sense of failure?

Additionally, due to the age difference between grandparents and their grandchildren, it is not uncommon for grandchildren to feel disconnected from their grandparents when it comes to issues like fashion, technology, leisure time, and social relationships. Expectations related to household rules and chores can also be sources of tension and conflict.

As Jaia Peterson Lent, deputy executive director of Generations United and a leading advocate for grandfamilies, writes in a 2018 *Aging Today* article on grandparents and the opioid crisis,

> One in five grandparents raising grandchildren lives below the poverty line. One in four has a disability. Most are thrust into the role suddenly: they are not prepared for that call in the middle of the night telling them to pick up the children or else they will end up in foster care. At a moment's notice, these grandparents are forced to navigate unfamiliar and complex systems to help meet the challenges of children who have come into their home, often after experiencing significant, sustained trauma. And the grandparents frequently face this unexpected challenge alone. They may suffer from social isolation and even depression because they do not want their peers to know about their situation or because their peers are no longer parenting. Caregivers of children whose parents are using drugs may

have their stress exacerbated by trying to maintain or navigate an ongoing relationship between the child and parent. As grandparent caregiver Chris Mathews explains in a 2016 Generations United report on the state of grandfamilies, "Grandparents are doing whatever it takes to bring their grandchildren to safety. We spend all of our savings. We lose our friends. We lose our identity."[1]

So how do we face these challenges? The following are a few obstacles we can expect to face and how to effectively deal with them.

Resentment

No matter how much you love your grandchildren, and especially if they are hard to love, taking them into your home and your life is not an uncomplicated change. It's one thing to be handling kids when their parents are doing something to be proud of and you've volunteered to help out. It's quite another when an adult child has failed as a parent and the grandkids are left on your doorstep.

Whatever the circumstances, most grandparents feel some combination of the following: resentment about the situation balanced by perhaps relief that a decision has been made; love for the grandchildren and anger and sadness about their parent or parents; and gratitude that they can provide for the kids with the genuine wish that they didn't feel they had to.

And that's okay. In fact, it's important to feel your feelings. The challenge is to not visit whatever negative feelings are in the mix on the children. After all, they are only children, and they are trying to manage their own feelings. It's not fair to ask them to manage yours as well. In addition, not only must we teach our grandchildren to forgive, but we must learn to forgive. Otherwise, the wounded become the wounders.

When people hear our story, they say things like how noble we are, or what a great thing we are doing by saving this child, or something similar. That is great and I appreciate their sentiments (although I'd rather they helped out with childcare or finances), but frankly I don't feel very noble. If I'm being honest, I more often feel overwhelmed and even a bit resentful because all my goals and dreams have been put on hold indefinitely (and at our age that might well be forever). After all, I already sacrificed everything to raise my own children. Now was supposed to be my time to travel around the world with my wife and fall in love with her all over again—to live life just for ourselves for a change.

And I resent the loss of my wife. She now spends all of her time, energy, and attention mothering this little person. I get only her leftovers, if that. Resentment for the hit to our sex life. A few years ago, I used to scoff when I heard young couples with small children complain about being too tired to have sex. Now I'm the one doing the complaining.

I resent being forced to be a disciplinarian when my natural role is to spoil her.

I resent the aging process. It felt like my wife and I were relatively young-looking and -feeling for our ages a few years ago. We were primed to be able to enjoy the beaches and mountains of the world. But the constant demands of a growing child are rapidly aging us physiologically—I can feel it and see it happening nearly daily in the mirror. And even some resentment at my deceased adult child for putting us in this situation to begin with (even though it certainly wasn't his choice).

I have resentment toward the Department of Human Services for being involved in our lives for more than three years. We had people invading our home weekly, often multiple times a week. Between court dates, visitations, and the stress associated with it all, my wife and I seldom had time to spend together. And that's not even considering all the diapers, crying, waking up at all hours of the night, etc. Now we have piano lessons, voice recitals, dance rehearsals, doctor appointments, sports practices, and parent-teacher conferences. And finally, there is the resentment, concern, and frankly fear of the financial burden and obligation placed upon us.

Wow! Sounds like I'm a cranky, cantankerous old man, doesn't it? Maybe so, but I'm just trying to be honest, because I suspect I'm not the only one who secretly harbors these emotions.

So how do we deal with resentment? We focus on our blessings! Attitude is everything. Recognizing and appreciating our blessings in life offsets any feelings of resentment and even bitterness. Do you have a loving spouse? Do you have a roof over your head and enough food to eat every day? Do you love your grandchildren? Are you relatively healthy? If you have even a few of those, you are luckier than most of the people in the world. By learning to lower our level of entitlement and even our expectations of what we deserve in life, we can be quite satisfied with what we have.

Financial Commitment

What does it cost to raise a child to adulthood now? About $250,000? What if you suddenly have two or three kids to raise? There goes retirement. As it is, I will be almost eighty years old when my little girl graduates from college (if she doesn't redshirt a year). I don't think I'll be retiring any time soon.

My biggest income-earning years are behind me. I doubt I could even get a job at my age. Thankfully, I am able to earn an income from my writing and speaking skills. I collect Social Security, and I also pick up odd jobs for extra income. Additionally, my wife has a good pension from her retirement. But many mature people depend solely upon Social Security or a small pension for their entire income. They didn't expect or anticipate that they would be raising another family in their later years. That makes providing for and raising children on a limited income very difficult.

While my wife and I have been blessed financially, several others we know have been forced to supplement their income or provisions through a variety of means. Many go to food banks at churches, nonprofit organizations, or social service agencies.

Some qualify for Special Supplemental Nutrition Program for Women, Infants, and Children (WIC), the Supplemental Nutrition Assistance Program (SNAP), or Temporary Assistance for Needy Families (TANF). Even though many of our generation were raised to despise taking government subsidies, if it comes to my children starving, I'm willing to swallow my pride and accept help wherever I can get it. There are a number of social service agencies and churches in every city that help those in need with food or other items that they cannot afford. We even had a nonprofit pay for a year of gymnastics tuition, which helped us immensely at the time.

Lastly, if you are able, jobs for people of our age are out there. They may not be as glamourous or as well-paying as we are used to, but they can be used to supplement other sources of income. Yeah, I'm not real thrilled about that prospect either, but again, if that's what you have to do, so be it. Besides writing and speaking, I tend to pick jobs I enjoy like substitute teaching, umpiring high school baseball games, and coaching high school basketball. These are part-time jobs I can do when I feel like it and when they fit into my schedule. Plus, they tend to keep me in good mental and physical condition.

Health

When we took custody of E, the state required us to take classes through the foster care system to get certified. Frankly, I was feeling a little sorry for myself as we began the classes because of the circumstances we found ourselves in. That is, until I spoke to the elderly couple next to us. In their mid-seventies, they were going to be raising three small children—their *great*-grandchildren! They quickly became an inspiration to me and my wife. Unfortunately, I found out a couple of years later that the man had died after falling off a ladder. (Doctor friends tell me ladders are the leading cause of injuries to men over fifty.)

What about health challenges? Having a kid in preschool is like being immersed in a petri dish containing every bacterium, virus, and germ known to mankind. Your grandchild's body then purifies it into a more virulent form of illness before passing it along to you.

The physical toll at our age is daunting as well. With our lower energy levels and lack of stamina, my wife and I go to bed exhausted each night. Our little eight-year-old now has more energy than any mammal on the planet. Her joyful shouts of, "Dad! Let's wrestle!" are more often than not met unenthusiastically as my creaking joints contort themselves down onto the hard floor. Her leaps off the sofa onto my aching back put me in the recliner for a week recuperating.

It's vitally important that we remain in good health. Daily exercise, eating right, and getting enough sleep are all important components of our physical and mental health. Remaining agile and flexible through stretching is invaluable as well. Lastly, getting respite from constant childrearing on a consistent basis is important for our psychological well-being.

Raising a child with emotional baggage can be quite burdensome and take an even greater toll on our health. Frequently, children from broken homes come with emotional baggage that can be difficult to navigate. Because of their experiences with their parents, "children being raised in grandparent-headed families may display a variety of developmental, physical, behavioral, academic, and emotional problems," says one family-service organization. Some of these problems include depression, anxiety, ADHD, health problems, separation anxiety, learning disabilities, poor academic performance, and aggression.[2]

We are dedicated to teaching our granddaughter independence at an early age. Hence, she is learning life skills sooner than many of her peers. She is learning to clean her room (an ongoing battle), vacuum, cook meals, and run the dishwasher. Beyond that, my wife is making a concentrated effort to teach her to can fruits and vegetables, bake a variety of foods, do laundry, and sew (all lost arts today). I'm making an effort to teach her how to fix things, do yardwork, pick up after the dog, and work on cars (change a tire and change the fluids), even at her young age. Thankfully, she is intelligent, with an inquisitive mind that makes teaching her easy, even if she does ask ten thousand questions. I'll soon start teaching her how to manage a household budget, pay bills, and mow the lawn.

Truth be told, we raised our own children to be a bit sheltered or even naïve. That's a luxury we cannot afford with our granddaughter. We are not young anymore, and if life has taught us anything, it's that things can change (or end) in a heartbeat. God forbid something happen to us with her totally unable to fend for herself. Our goal is that by age sixteen, she will be totally self-sufficient.

That said, it's important, if not imperative, that you have a will which nominates a caregiver for your grandchildren should you die. Leaving your grandchildren to become wards of the state in the event of your passing is irresponsible, if not reprehensible. Again, if you do not have an attorney, there are organizations that can provide these services for little or no cost. At the very least, you can download the forms for free off the internet.

Lower Stamina and Energy

Anyone out there have more stamina and energy than you did thirty years ago? There's a good reason why the prime child-bearing years are eighteen to twenty-eight and not sixty. I sometimes watch old videotapes of my wife slinging around two active toddlers, and I'm amazed at her energy level as a young woman (not to mention how gorgeous she was). I can distinctly remember how, as a young father, I would spend hours wrestling on the floor or playing games with the kids. Now I'm lucky to get up off the floor at all once I get down there. I might rouse up the energy for a quick game of tag, but I'm forced to take a nap afterward.

However, raising a young child actually does keep me in shape. Have you ever tried to catch a runaway toddler in a store or playground? It's like trying to catch the Gingerbread Man. They are slippery as eels. How can they run so fast on those short little legs anyway? They have the uncanny ability to barely move a shoulder or hip an instant before you can reach out and grab them, causing you to trip and stumble even as they totter along, barely keeping their balance, their big old melons bent forward in a headlong rush. If an NFL running back had the moves of a toddler, they would lead the league in rushing every year.

However, all that said, there are some huge benefits to raising these little treasures, as we will find out in the following chapter.

CHAPTER 4

Advantages of Raising Children Later in Life

What children need most are the essentials that grand-parents provide in abundance. They give unconditional love, kindness, patience, humor, comfort, lessons in life. And, most importantly, cookies.

—Rudy Giuliani

A variety of studies in the U.S. on the development of children's well-being in those raised by grandparents have had mixed findings. However, they do reveal that some of these children have impaired well-being compared to children living with their parents, due to factors such as exposure to drugs both in utero and afterwards or suffering from physical, emotional, or sexual abuse. Those children also often have learning and behavioral disorders. In such circumstances, it's difficult to quantify just how positive or negative the grandparents' influence may have been. But in general, "grandchildren raised by grandparents tend to fare better than [those] raised by single parents or those in foster care."[1] In fact, "children being raised solely by grand-parents appear to be relatively healthy and well-adjusted."[2]

According to a 2017 article published in *U.S. News*, "Grand-parents provide stability, safety, wisdom, and fun for kids. In return, caring for grandchildren can help stave off depression, boost social connections and keep older adults mentally sharp."[3] Moreover, according to a June 2016 study from Boston University, "emotional closeness between adult grandchildren and their grandparents protects against depression for both." Another study showed that spending quality time with grand-children improves mental health and brain function, lowering depression in older people. One study even suggested that caring for grandchildren leads to longer life.[4]

While it might seem that there are only disadvantages to raising a family later in life, there are also plenty of compelling benefits that make it easier than it was the first time around. Here are just a few:

More Powerful Love. Every night when our granddaughter goes to bed, she says as part of her prayers, " . . . and God bless Mom and Dad, especially Mom. . . ." The first time I heard her say that, I almost burst out laughing. Then I thought, "Wait, what am I, chopped liver?" But it makes sense that at her age she would value Grandma's essence more than mine. After all, she brings more to the table. She cooks, cleans, nurtures, and loves our grand-daughter unconditionally. I'm a bit more performance-based in my love, and E is not yet old enough yet to recognize my contribu-tions of providing for and protecting her in all areas of her life. Grandmothers by nature are "fixers." If someone is hurt or upset, they want to make them better. If someone is hungry or cold, they feed and nurture them.

My wife's Nana was a little old lady with a club foot who'd been crippled by polio as a child. Yet she was one of the most inspirational people I ever met. Though she was poor and lived on a Social Security pension, she faithfully tithed to a church that she never attended because she was housebound. Over the years, she took in stray kids (including my wife), feeding them soup made from chicken carcasses and sandwiches made with cheese so thin you could see through it. She sewed quilts her entire life, sending them to missionaries around the world. And last, but not least, she prayed for my soul daily for sixteen years until I finally became a Christian at age forty.

The very nature of grandparents dictates that we are freer to love our grandchildren more unconditionally than parents often are. For one thing, there's no parental pressure causing us to think that the choices our kids make are a direct reflection upon us. This can be beneficial emotionally and psychologically for both child and grandparent.

One researcher put it this way:

> As I interviewed grandfamilies across New York, the thing that struck me the most was the great warmth and appreciation grandparents and grandchildren have for each other and how much they value the important role that they play in each other's lives.[5]

Taking custody of our granddaughter after the death of our son was a double-edged sword. On one hand, while having to help her through her grief and trauma made it difficult for us to properly process our own, it also kept me from dwelling too much on my loss. The one true blessing is that E's love for me and my love for her has had a cathartic effect in helping me heal from that loss.

In fact, she may have even saved my life. Without the responsibility of raising her, I would have been very tempted to end my life in my grief and sorrow. Not only that, but she has brought a joy and love of life that I get to experience from a fresh perspective. She makes me laugh out loud many times every day. Her exuberance and excitement over life is a salve to my old, jaded soul. I don't know if that has kept me young, but it certainly has been fun. Now, I can't imagine not having her in my life.

More Patience. Typically, as we get older, we develop more patience. I know some of us become crusty old blokes and pinched old biddies, but generally, life's experiences help us recognize what is really important in the world. What we should have discovered by our fifth or sixth decade is that families and relationships are what matter most in life.

I'm not the most patient man on the planet (I've never suffered fools lightly), but I do have more patience with my granddaughter than I ever did with my kids. I allow her to fail. I've learned over the years that failing is actually good—it's how we learn. I was a lot more intense as a first-time father, probably confusing my kids' performance with the quality of my parenting. Or maybe I just have less testosterone now, which makes me less aggressive and competitive.

More Experience. Even though I don't remember a lot of what went on daily while raising our first set of kids, I do have a lot more experience now than I did then. I've hopefully learned from the things that caught me off guard the first time. Having already raised two children, I know a lot more about how kids behave, how they react to situations, and what they try to get away with. Couple that with the fact that I've got a few more years of wisdom under my belt, and I'm better prepared to raise a child this time than I was before. And you are, too.

More Resources. Even though my wife and I are not rich, we do have a lot more resources than we did as younger parents. We have paid-off cars, savings, retirement investments, a fully furnished home, a monthly Social Security income, pension income, insurance, and all of the accoutrements that go along with having lived a full life. We had none of those things when our first set of children were young. We were just starting out together in life, trying to raise a family and get ahead. Our budget was stretched thin, and we had to make do without many things back then.

In addition, some of our resources are intangible in nature. We have a wealth of life experience and the wisdom that comes with that. We've made plenty of mistakes along the way, and now we can reap the rewards of having learned.

While many grandparents struggle financially with raising grandchildren, many of us are also better off than we were as young parents.

More Time. Part of the reason I don't remember a lot of the day-to-day events from raising our first family is because I was working all the time. My wife was home with the kids all day while I was gone. They even went on vacation for three weeks one year while I stayed at home (not something I would choose to do again if I could do it over). But as a small business owner, it seemed like we never had the money and/or time together to do big vacations or trips. When we had money, it was because we were busy at work and I had to be there. When I had the time to go, it was because business was slow—and that meant I didn't have the money to go on a vacation.

Now, being semi-retired, I have both time and money to do pretty much whatever we want when we want to do it. It's become increasingly apparent that what really matters in relationships are shared experiences.

Character

After a certain age, it's easy to become set in our ways. Especially if you haven't had children around for a while, it's easy to forget what kind of a role model you want to be to those "always watching" little eyes. Luckily, the Bible offers some pretty clear advice on how we are supposed to conduct ourselves as elders in the community of life. In these verses, Paul clearly places the responsibility of moral leadership on the elders. If the lives of grandparents demonstrated the following traits, they would leave a lasting impact on following generations. Here's what that should look like:

Grandfathers

Titus 2:2 admonishes seasoned men to "temperate, dignified, self-controlled, sound in faith, in love, in perseverance" (NASB). Here, it seems to me that Titus is speaking about men over the age of fifty, but "maturity is never determined by age. It is determined by how skilled a person is in applying truth to life and in distinguishing good from evil" (NKJV).[6] Let's break down each of the character traits Titus says men should exhibit.

"Temperate" or "sober" generally means "not drunk on alcohol." However, the Bible uses it to mean something of a spiritual nature. "Sober" in this sense comes from the Greek word *sophron,* meaning "of a sound and well-balanced mind; moderate, prudent, sensible, reasonable."[7] Examples might be moderate in the indulgences of appetites and passions, in pleasures, and in speech. Cool and calm, not violent. Sober in judgment, self-controlled, steady and balanced; vigilant; a man not ruled by his appetites. All things men need to be in order to lead our families well.

"Dignified and self-controlled" can also be interpreted as reverent, which means to show fear and deep, solemn respect for God. A man who is reverent is likely to be dignified and sensible—prudent in his choices, rational in his opinions, and wise in his decisions.

"Sound in faith" means trusting in God and having an honest, personal daily relationship with the Lord. Courageous faith stays true despite difficult circumstances (including the loss of a loved one). A man's faith (whatever form that takes or lacks) is always transmitted to his heirs. Faith is belief not based on proof. It is confidence in something you cannot see, hear, or smell. It is intangible, not subject to material evidence. It is loyalty, fidelity, and trust in God and His teachings. For example, I believe there is an omnipotent God who created the universe and everything in it, even though I cannot prove His existence by any scientific manner.

I've recently met several children who had terminal illnesses. Following their journey and those of their parents as they walked through the Valley of the Shadow of Death has been a hugely expansive experience in my life and for my faith. All those family members have been people of great faith. Their courage and steadfast faith have inspired thousands of others. One little girl's battle with cancer was documented in emails to friends and family. Her courageous faith in the most horrendous circumstances was awe-inspiring. Her parents' questions, concerns, and hearts crying out to God had me blubbering in tears every time I read their reports. Frankly, I know of no more courageous people than those who suffer the death of their child and are still able to come through the experience with their faith unshaken and intact.

"Sound in love" means being grounded and steady in your love for your wife and children. I made a lot of mistakes as a father (and still do), but one thing my kids have never had to question is whether I love them. That means we speak love into those under our care and make sure our actions prove it. My wife has stated that over the years I've said many things that made her angry, but when she stopped and thought about it, my actions always showed I loved her.

Love is a virtue or emotion representing all of human kindness, compassion, and affection. Love may refer to the passionate desire and intimacy of romantic love, to sexual love, to the emotional closeness of familial love, or to the platonic love that defines friendship. Perhaps the greatest attribute of love is its willingness to sacrifice for the benefit of another. Husbands and wives sacrifice for each other in healthy marriages. Parents make sacrifices for their children all the time, giving up personal gratifications for the good of the child. And grandparents like you make huge sacrifices to save the lives of their grandchildren.

According to Google, "patience" is "the capacity to accept or tolerate delay, trouble, or suffering without getting angry or upset." A man's anger, while often comfortable to him, can be very frightening to women and children. Being calm and consistent are traits we should strive for.

One of the things I have learned over the course of my lifetime is to only be concerned about the things over which I have control. It takes too much emotional energy to worry about the things which are beyond my control. I've spent a large part of my life worrying about "what if?" kinds of things. But it serves no purpose, and most of those things I was worrying about never came to fruition anyway. It was a waste of my time and energy.

While not specifically mentioned in Titus 2:2, the Bible mentions wisdom as being a necessity in several other verses, including 2 Chronicles 1:10, Job 28:18, and Proverbs 2:12. Wisdom enables a man to do the right thing for the right reason at the right time. Brett and Kate McKay write in an April 2020 article on The Art of Manliness website that

> Socrates believed that man's purpose in life was to seek *sophia,* or wisdom. According to Socrates and his student, Plato, achieving *sophia* gave a man a general understanding of the nature of virtue. And once a man reached an understanding of each of the virtues, he would naturally live them out. For example, if a man understood the true nature of justice, he would naturally be just.[8]

The good thing about wisdom is it is generally obtained through experience—something guys who have been around the block a time or two have in abundance.

Grandmothers

For mature women, Titus 2:3–5 states, "that they be reverent in behavior, not slanderers, not given to too much wine, teachers of good things—that they admonish the young women to love their husbands, to love their children, to be discreet, chaste, homemakers, good, obedient to their husbands" (NKJV).

These verses encourage older women not to engage in evil activities such as gossip or drunkenness, but to teach younger women the important things in life. To pass on their insights to their younger counterparts. According to the New King James Version Bible Commentary, the word "admonish" here means to "give encouragement through advice."[9] When Paul said they should "love their husbands," it was not romantic love he spoke of, but the commitment of a woman to her husband's welfare and well-being.[10]

For women, "reverent in behavior" (as the GW translation terms it) means to live their lives in a way that shows they are dedicated to God.[11]

Not being a malicious gossip, in my opinion, means she is humble and has a Christlike love for her neighbors. A mature woman understands that spreading gossip does great damage to those around her and those under her influence.

Finally, older women are called upon to teach younger women the important things in life. This includes being discreet (not a gossip, but holding secrets safe), being chaste (abstaining from sexual immorality), and loving their husbands and children.

When my wife and I were newlyweds, I first met her Nana. I had been told she was a strong Christian woman. Not a believer at that time, and in fact never yet having been exposed to anyone who was, I wasn't sure what to expect. Imagine my surprise and delight when every time my new bride and I got into an argument and she ran to Nana to complain about me, Nana would only say, "Oh honey, just love him. Just love him." Straight out of Titus 2.

It was pretty frustrating for my wife at the time, but a welcome relief to a young man who grew up in an alcoholic family that delighted in blaming everyone around them and verbally tearing each other down.

"Not being enslaved to too much wine" means not being dependent upon controlled substances. For single women, loneliness and depression can grind away at their happiness and zap the joy out of life. For some, alcohol and chemical dependency can relieve some of those feelings. In addition, the aches and pains of age can cause some people to become addicted to pain relievers. Those types of actions and/or addictions not only are detrimental to our health, they can also model the wrong example for our grandchildren.

CHAPTER 5

Outcomes of Kids Raised by Grandparents

As your kids grow up, they may forget what you said,
but they won't forget how you made them feel.

—Kevin Heath

Frequently, we only hear the horror stories about grandparents raising their grandchildren, but in reality both kids and grands benefit from this relationship. Despite the higher-than-normal numbers of kids with emotional and behavioral problems being raised by grandparents, most in these circumstances do well, thank you very much. And they tend to be grateful for the sacrifices their grandparents have made.

It's important to remember that all of our stories involve traumatic circumstances on some level. However, to my mind, all of our stories are success stories because we have literally rescued and even saved the lives of these children.

Positive Outcomes

Mona (not her real name) was a physician's assistant working in the trauma unit at a local hospital whom I interviewed for this book in late 2020. Her teenage daughter had run away from home and gotten involved in drugs. She then got pregnant and bore a three-pound, five-ounce baby who was addicted to methamphetamine and suffering from fetal alcohol syndrome. After going through a neonatal intensive care unit program, state authorities took custody of the baby and offered her to Mona to raise. She immediately quit her job to be a full-time mother to this special-needs child.

Over the next four years, Mona's daughter had two more drug-addicted babies, whom Mona adopted as well. All three girls had intense issues to deal with, due to drug exposure in the womb. The oldest was born with swallowing issues, causing her to gag, aspirate, and throw up nearly every time she ate. She also had receptive-expressive language skills, which caused her to strike out when she couldn't express herself. One of the other girls suffered from a condition where she could not protect herself when she lost her balance. Once, she fell on her face and lost both her front teeth.

All three girls suffered from precocious puberty, meaning their pituitary glands secreted adult hormones at an early age, manifesting in the development of breasts and armpit hair. They also suffered from muscle flaccidity, meaning their muscles were limp and unable to contract—so learning to walk required intense physical therapy. And none were able to accept any hugging, touching, or physical contact due to their sensory conditions.

While Mona's story would seem hopeless, nothing could be further from the truth. With a positive, can-do spirit she worked tirelessly with the girls, entering them into as many physical therapy programs, mental health sessions, and medical appointments as possible—all free through a local county program she discovered. She also had high expectations for the girls; she considered their issues to be "glitches." She told the girls that everyone has glitches in their lives, and they had to learn to overcome them.

Today, the girls are nineteen, eighteen, and fifteen years old. The oldest has a full-time job and was recently offered a full four-year scholarship to college. Despite her sensory issues, she recently was able to hold her boyfriend's hand and even kiss him! All three girls are proficient in playing multiple musical instruments. The eighteen-year-old is a drum majorette in her high school band and aspires to be a French teacher.[1]

Quite a journey from where they started. Not to put too fine a point on it, but one dedicated grandmother not only saved the lives of three girls, but also prepared them to live healthy, happy, and fulfilling lives of their own. Mona is one of my heroes.

Like the girls in the story, research suggests many children develop strong relationships with their grandparents and are grateful for their love and support. These children say their "grandparents' love and stability allowed them to succeed in school, stay out of trouble, develop strong morals, and religious values."[2]

As stated previously, being raised by a grandparent can yield several benefits for grandchildren. The American Association for Marriage and Family Therapy (AAMFT) lists some of these as "greater stability and safety, the maintenance of relationships with siblings and extended family members, and the continuation of cultural identity and community ties."[3] That said, the path ahead is often fraught with peril.

Issues to Be Aware Of

I interviewed numerous grandparents raising their grandchildren as I was writing this book. Just as most single parents are women, most of the grandparents raising their grandchildren are single women. Most of the stories about how they became involved in these circumstances were very similar as well: drug abuse by the parents and subsequent neglect of the children seemed to be the biggest factor in the grandchildren being removed from their homes.

For example, according to an article from the Michigan Psychological Association, "children in grandparent-led households are six times more likely to have had a parent or guardian serve time in jail, and four times more likely to have lived with someone who has a drug or alcohol problem."[4]

Additionally, a significant amount of these children appear to suffer from maladies stemming from the abuse they experienced. These include being needy, having high anxiety, control issues, attention-deficit hyperactivity disorder, learning disorders, separation anxiety, reactive attachment disorder, post-traumatic stress disorder, depression, landing somewhere on the autism spectrum, being diagnosed as oppositional-defiant, having abandonment issues, bedwetting, and other emotional and behavioral disorders. Many kids also experience trauma from having gone through the "system" of foster care or even state-sponsored adoption. One study conducted in Norway concluded that 50 percent of kids between the ages of six and twelve in foster care suffer from one or more of the above-mentioned disorders.[5]

An American study examined the differences between children in foster care versus those in the general population. Using data from the 2011–2012 National Survey of Children's Health, it showed that children placed in foster care (whether being raised by family members or not) were twice as likely to have learning disabilities, developmental delays, asthma, obesity, and speech problems. They were three times more likely to have ADD/ADHD, five times more likely to have anxiety, six times more likely to have behavioral problems, and seven times more likely to have depression.[6]

All that to say that grandparents raising grandchildren face some unique and even challenging circumstances when raising wounded kids. Let's look at some of those challenges and how they can be overcome.

Benefits of Grandparents Raising Grandchildren

Amy is a girl I interviewed for this book. She was two weeks old when her mother was killed in a car accident. Nearly two years later, her father died in a boating accident. Because her maternal grandparents were struggling with addictions, Amy was adopted by her paternal grandparents; she called them her "parents," and they always tried to make sure she lived as normal a life as possible. That included ensuring she was surrounded by family (she fondly remembers spending parts of her summers with her aunt and uncle and eight cousins), keeping her immersed in activities with other children, and doing plenty of other things together. She and grandma gardened together a lot. She credits her grandma (the most kind-hearted woman she's ever met) with teaching her to always treat people with kindness. Her grandpa was rougher around the edges. Ex-military, he was strict, and they butted heads frequently as she got older. Amy felt like she had to live up to the high expectations her grandfather set for her. But from him she gleaned a strong work ethic (she worked two jobs in high school) as well as the knowledge that if she put her mind to it, she could accomplish anything. Their relationship bloomed after high school when her grandpa shared how proud he was of her and that he loved her just the way she was.

Her grandmother was terribly emotionally wounded when her only son passed away. She told Amy that she probably would not have survived if it weren't for the fact that Amy brought so much joy into her life. Grandmother also admitted to her that she often felt like a failure as a mother to Amy, not being able to do all the things a younger mother could. But Amy said knowing she had someone who didn't hesitate to drop everything to take her in and give her everything possible was such a blessing. She is thankful and grateful for her grandparents and loves them dearly.

Tips for Raising Grandchildren[7]

- Plan a daily routine of mealtimes, bedtime, and other activities so that the kids learn to have some certainty and stability in their lives.
- Make them feel at home by giving them a place to call their own, like giving them their own room for their belongings. Make your home welcoming, safe, and child friendly.
- Take special care of younger grandkids by providing nutritious food.
- Read to them every day.
- Keep their immunization up to date.
- Communicate with your grandchildren and ensure they know they can talk to you whenever they feel like it, because poor communication leads to relationship problems later in life.
- Help grandchildren practice safety by being a role model (for instance, always eat your meals at the table, buckle your seatbelt, etc.).
- Make a few rules, explain them to the children, and enforce them consistently but lovingly.
- Where your grandchildren's living parents are concerned, set a good example by peacefully working out arguments.
- Seek out appropriate services as soon as possible if your grandchild has special needs.
- Monitor movies, music, television, and the use of computers.
- Most importantly, make your grandchild feel loved, important, and cared for. And don't forget to spend good family time with them.

Today, Amy is enrolled in nursing school with the goal of becoming a pediatric nurse. Looking back, she feels truly blessed that the Lord put her grandparents in her life.[9]

Despite the high rate of emotional and behavioral problems traumatized kids experience, one psychotherapist cites a University of Oxford study showing that those who have close

The Importance of Family Rituals for Traumatized Kids—Especially during the Holidays

An Oregon support group for grandfamilies posted the following on its Facebook page on December 9, 2020.[8]

- *Value family rituals.* Rituals help us connect with each other, ease pain, and move from one place to another. For children who have experienced loss and trauma, participating in family rituals can be a critical part of healing. Be thoughtful about what rituals children may have had during the holidays before they came to live with you, and which they may want to continue. It's also okay to set aside aspects of rituals that are painful to continue. A therapist can work with you and the child to identify ways to continue or adapt past rituals in a healthy way.
- *Give permission to feel sad.* Holidays are a time for celebration. They can also bring up painful memories, feelings of loss, or even anger toward other family members. Let your grandchild know it's okay to feel sad sometimes, and that you feel sad too. Spending some time together talking about your feelings can release tension and help you both enjoy and celebrate your holiday traditions.
- *Create new traditions.* Traditions give children a sense of comfort and connection, and something special to look forward to. You can start new traditions even while respecting those from your grandchild's previous family arrangements. Begin making a new kind of cookie together, take a special trip, or share a toy and play a game together that you loved during the holidays as a child.
- *Offer simple and shared food.* Holiday meals don't have to be elaborate sit-down dinners to feel festive. Most children (and plenty of adults) will enjoy fun-cut carrot sticks and snowman-shaped cheese sandwiches over a pot roast any day. If you do want a sit-down meal, invite your friends and family, but encourage them to bring a dish to share.

- *Get crafty.* From Etsy to Pinterest, the internet is bursting with low-cost ideas for presents, décor, and entertaining, even for those who don't fancy themselves a Martha Stewart.
- *Decorate with Mother Nature.* Decorate your tree with strings of popcorn, your front door with branches and leaves from your yard, or make an artful centerpiece using acorns and stones.
- *Give the gift of time.* Promise to do a chore for a friend or family member; gift a foot rub or massage, or even a night of your undivided attention to play a game of his/her choice with each of your grandchildren.
- *Connect with a caring community.* During this season, communities often abound with food and holiday gift drives to help families needing a little boost. Find out what is available in your community and how to sign up, if it's a good match for you.

relationships with their grandparents have fewer of them, and less difficulty dealing with their peers.[10]

According to an article titled "Development of Well-Being in Children Raised by Grandparents," studies on the topic have had mixed findings. For instance, kids in their grandparents' custody have greater risk of psychological, behavioral, health, and academic problems than children in the general population.[11] But in general, the outcomes of children raised by grandparents are not significantly different from those raised in traditional homes; they actually have better physical health and fewer behavioral problems than children living with one biological parent.[12]

The following story comes from a young man whom I interviewed for this book:

Paul's parents split up when he was young. His father wasn't the most engaged man on the planet before that, but he became even less involved with his son after the divorce. When he was engaged, he tended to be abusive. Consequently, Paul needed a positive male role model in his life.

While Paul did not live exclusively with his grandparents, he did spend most summers with them before finally moving in full-time for several years in high school and while in college. He fondly remembers beach vacations and camping. He credits his grandparents—especially his grandfather, Poppy—with teaching him the most important lessons in life. He spent a lot of time with Poppy working on cars, working the farm, and fishing. He describes his grandfather as a "man's man." He quickly bonded with a man willing to share his time and wisdom. Paul says his grandfather gave him a softer kind of love. Besides the great amounts of wisdom his grandfather applied, he also shared with him other things in life, like the importance of holiday traditions.[13]

Paul's memories of that time with his grandparents are filled with love, fun, laughter, and plenty of good food. Today, as a successful health care professional and young newlywed, he claims the biggest gift they gave him was the example of a playful, loving marriage and relationship—something he had not experienced before.

The good news is that children raised by grandparents can and do thrive. Compared to children in foster care with non-relatives, those raised by caring relatives appear to have more successful long-term outcomes.[14] In fact, grandparents and other relatives have a special protective role with these children that helps to mitigate trauma.

So take heart! Your presence in your grandchildren's lives matters, even if it doesn't feel like it sometimes. Grandfathers can be especially important to kids without fathers, as we'll see in the next chapter.

CHAPTER 6

Why Grandfathers Matter

*My father gave me the greatest gift anyone could give
another person: He believed in me.*

—Jim Valvano

Much like fathers, it's difficult to overemphasize the importance of a grandfather in a child's life. Grandpa, whether
you believe it or not, or whether you even want the responsibility or not, if you are raising your grandchild, you are fulfilling the role of a father. Absent or abusive fathers cause a
lifetime of problems for both boys and girls. But the good side
to that is the love and presence of a good man cures the wounds
left by a bad man. I've seen it happen nearly every day in the
mentoring ministry we operate for fatherless boys. Grandma,
if you are raising your grandchildren alone, it's imperative to
recognize the importance of involving positive male role models
in the lives of your grandchildren.

One of the effects of being fatherless is that boys often try to
feel like men through the sexual conquest of girls or women. And

Traits of an Excellent Father/Grandfather

- Demonstrates love
- Keeps his promises
- Loves his spouse
- Models excellent character
- Understands the needs of his children
- Trains his children in life skills
- Sacrifices for his children
- Doesn't quit

the effect of fatherlessness on girls is just as damaging: They long to fill the void of nonsexual affection, but often seek to do so through sexual encounters with boys or men. Fatherless kids have a father-sized hole in their souls. The tempter tries to fill that hole with temptation. Drug dealers, pimps, and hustlers know fathers matter. I once heard a pastor say he talked to a pimp who told him, "The first question I ask a girl is, 'Do you have a father?' If she says no, I know I got her."

Let me talk briefly about some of the outcomes of boys and girls raised without positive male role models in their lives—not because female role models are any less important, but because it's the most common scenario we see. Nationally, about 80 percent of single parents are female, and nearly half of all babies are born to single moms.[1] Of the dozens of grandparents raising grandchildren whom I interviewed for this book, only two were not single grandmothers.

Perhaps the two greatest gifts a man provides to a child are provision and protection. And indeed, both are hugely important in a child's life. How frightening is it for a helpless child to face the evils of the world with no protection? Or to be homeless, not knowing where the next meal will come from? Men are uniquely qualified to provide both of those gifts to children, but they are also necessary for a host of other things that are specific to each gender.

Girls

Grandpa, if a girl's biological father is not involved in her life or is a poor role model that has done great damage, you have a big task ahead of you. Girls without dads face a plethora of challenges. They are often broken and hurt. Thankfully, you've already been through the parenting game, so you have some experience and wisdom to offer.

Girls without fathers (or healthy father substitutes) are much more likely to engage in sexually promiscuous behavior at an early age, become unwed teenage mothers, drop out of high school, and have worse academic performance than those with fathers. They are also more likely to experience poverty, physical, emotional, and psychological abuse, use drugs or alcohol, and become a victim of crime.[2]

But beyond the physical risks, girls without fathers suffer psychological disadvantages as well. Girls deprived of a father's love and affection make poor choices in an effort to fill that void. Sometimes this means connecting with a man who has the same qualities as her father—for example, a woman who was verbally abused by her father will often choose a verbally

Effects of Fatherlessness

- An estimated 24.7 million children (33 percent) live without their biological father.[3]
- Children in father-absent homes are almost four times more likely to be poor. In 2011, 12 percent of children in married-couple families were living in poverty, compared to 44 percent of children in mother-only families.[4]
- Children living in female-headed families with no spouse present had a poverty rate of 47.6 percent, over four times the rate in married-couple families.[5]
- The U.S. Department of Health and Human Services (DHHS) states, "Fatherless children are at a dramatically greater risk of drug and alcohol abuse."[6]
- Data from three waves of the Fragile Families Study was used to examine the prevalence and effects of mothers' relationship changes between birth and age three on their children's well-being. Children born to single mothers show higher levels of aggressive behavior than children born to married mothers. Living in a single-mother household is equivalent to experiencing 5.25 partnership transitions.[7]
- According to a 2012 article in *Psychology Today*, "71 percent of high school dropouts are fatherless; fatherless children have more trouble academically, scoring poorly on tests of reading, mathematics, and thinking skills; children from father-absent homes are more likely to play truant from school, more likely to be excluded from school, more likely to leave school at age 16, and less likely to attain academic and professional qualifications in adulthood."[8]
- Children aged ten to seventeen living with two biological or adoptive parents were significantly less likely to experience sexual assault or other types of major violence and were less likely to witness violence in their families compared to peers living in single-parent families and stepfamilies.[9]
- Being raised by a single mother raises the risk of teen pregnancy, marrying with less than a high school degree, and forming a marriage where both partners have less than a high school degree.[10]

abusive partner. In her book *Women and Their Fathers*, Victoria Secunda discusses another theme common among women who did not have a father: the inability to trust that a man won't eventually abandon her. "Counting on and loving a man is a leap of faith, because for them a 'permanent relationship' is an entirely theoretical" construct. These women "tend to test the men in their lives by starting fights, finding flaws, or expecting to be abandoned"—and that belief system, coupled with those behaviors, often leads to self-fulfilling prophecy.[11]

One day when my daughter was in high school, I came home from work early. She had stayed home sick and was watching a TV show about young women training to be models. In this episode, the participants were learning to cry on command. The instructor passed out a piece of notebook paper to each girl with the following instructions: "I want you to pretend this is a letter from your father saying he is leaving you and never coming back." All of the girls were visibly distraught and crying as the impact of what they were told dawned on them.

The instructor then said, "Now I want you to take out your anger on your father by destroying the letter." All of the girls had an instantaneous, visceral reaction and tore the paper into small pieces, some screaming in rage. I was stunned. Either all of those young women were already accomplished actresses, or it was a powerful example of a father's importance in a girl's life.

Girls who do not receive healthy masculine love and affection from their fathers crave it throughout their lives. Many women either willingly substitute or confuse sex for love in their desire for masculine affection. Father-deprived girls show precocious sexual interest and have less ability to maintain sexual and emotional adjustment with just one male. Without a father, a girl must learn about boys without a man's perspective. They are like lambs without a shepherd. Without a father's influence and guidance, even the most normal male activities may seem bizarre and strange. By contrast, daughters who have had the benefit of healthy father involvement are more independent and self-possessed, and they are more likely to assume responsibility for the consequences of their actions.[12]

In her book *Do You Think I'm Beautiful?*, Angela Thomas writes,

> I can be in a small group of women and tell you in a matter of moments which ones have had a healthy, loving relationship with their fathers. There is a certain confidence and peace that comes from a woman who has known such love. And there is an anxiousness and insecurity buried inside a woman who has never known a father's love or, worse, who has suffered wounds from his words or his distance or his hands.[13]

Women who have been hurt deeply in some way by their fathers tend to either take that pain out on men throughout their lifetimes or become victims of men.

Any child deprived of his or her God-given right to a father suffers from father hunger. Father-deprived girls tend to internalize their pain and harm themselves. Your daughter/granddaughter desperately needs you in her life, no matter how young or old she may be.

Boys

Several years ago, we began presenting seminars for women on raising boys to become good men. The seminars are for mothers, grandmothers, aunts, teachers and administrators, social workers, and any other women who work or live with boys. But we found a huge segment of our culture where women were being forced to raise sons on their own and were desperate to understand what their sons needed to grow into good men. Many of these women faced big disadvantages raising boys and understanding what their sons needed, not only by not being male themselves, but by not having been raised with a father or brothers while growing up. After presenting enough of these seminars, it became clear that one of the biggest challenges these moms faced was not having positive male role models available in their sons' lives.

In response to this dilemma, we started a program called Standing Tall—a mentoring program for fatherless boys similar to a faith-based Big Brothers program. It originally started in partnership with a local Bible college. There we trained male seminary students to spend a couple of hours a week with fatherless boys identified through our seminars for moms. Almost immediately we started seeing some startling results. Mothers of the boys began reporting changes in their sons' entire countenances. Their sons were better behaved, less angry, more respectful of them, and doing better in school. Some credited the presence of the mentors with their sons' improvement in reading scores (even though they never read together). They noted behavioral changes such as the cessation of bedwetting. Nearly all of the boys experienced more self-confidence and composure during their daily life activities.

We teach the mentors to use physical activities with the boys. Many fatherless boys spend large amounts of unsupervised time in front of the television or video games, which is unhealthy on so many levels. We encourage them to proactively use "teaching" opportunities for things like driving nails, catching baseballs, shooting basketball hoops, riding a bike, using a pocketknife safely, hiking in the wilderness, and so forth—all the things that boys without dads do not learn and therefore feel inadequate in. We sometimes teach older boys skills such as shaving and other appropriate personal hygiene tips. You might be surprised at the simplest things you or I take for granted that fatherless boys do not know how to do. And because it is embarrassing to ask, they often stumble through life without ever getting that knowledge.

We encourage the mentors to intentionally teach character traits such as self-discipline, perseverance (not quitting), honesty, courage, and respect for women and others. Many of these boys do not learn these character traits—not because mothers don't value them, but because they are more readily learned and accepted coming from an older male.

Another issue we observe in fatherless boys is the unwilling-
ness to accept challenges. Because they have no confidence and
a reluctance to experience humiliation through their failures,
many of these boys do not receive the valuable lessons and
self-esteem garnered from failing and persevering until they succeed. They also become frustrated and quit anything the first
time it becomes difficult. They tend to cry easier than most boys.
When they fall down and scrape a knee, they will instantly cry
and wait for Mom to come rescue them. If a man picks them up
and dusts them off, they recognize they are not really hurt and
stop crying right away. Again, a male's presence helps to guide
and encourage them to persevere until they succeed, thereby
gaining the positive self-image and confidence to accept risk and
attempt challenges in other areas of life.

Another observation we make of fatherless boys is the propensity they all have to be somewhat "different." I don't use the
term "different" in a disparaging manner, but many (if not most)
of these boys seem to have some sort of disadvantage associated
with them. It might consist of behavioral problems, speech
impediments, emotional struggles, or even learning disabilities
(frequently attributable to ADHD), but they generally have some
sort of physical or emotional "issue" that sets them apart from
their peers. Often these differences cause them to be isolated and
more comfortable in female company, which tends to be more
compassionate and accepting. They tend to have trouble fitting
in with their peer group. Because of the lack of male role models,
they have adapted to being around only women. This makes

them uncomfortable around males. This propensity also makes them easier prey to fall in with any social group that does accept them, such as gangs of other fatherless boys or unhealthy male role models of all types.

These observations are purely anecdotal on my part, but various studies appear to support the emotional struggles boys have without a father. The trauma and stress of losing their father, possibly combined with having only female influences in their life, manifests itself through a variety of problems.

In a study Rogers Wright and Nicholas Cummings describe in their book *Destructive Trends in Mental Health: The Well-Intentioned Path to Harm*, kids with ADHD were paired with male therapists due to the noted absence of father involvement in the children's lives. All of the boys and girls in the study were on medication for their malady. During the study, the kids were given behavioral treatment with the therapists, and special attention was paid to developing a positive attachment to the male figure. At the end of the treatment, only 11 percent of the boys and 2 percent of the girls had to remain on medication.[14] My organization, Better Dads Ministries, works with people to help them break negative generational cycles. My volunteers and I have found in our work that all positive male role models are effective in reducing or eliminating problems in boys without fathers involved in their lives.

A boy needs a father to be a role model for life for him. It's not that he is perfect and never makes mistakes. I certainly made many mistakes as a father, husband, and man and continue to do so. But the effort is important. A son who sees his father try to be the best role model possible is inspired by the effort itself—especially if the father admits his mistakes and learns from them. Many a boy was inspired by his father's example of manliness under pressure. Likewise, many have been dismayed or even destroyed by their father's absence or abuse. Manhood and fatherhood are learned behaviors. Boys are visual creatures and learn by observing. By watching how men react in certain situations, what they say, and how they solve problems, boys learn to become men. Boys need to be instructed at an early age to take on their manly responsibilities.

For fatherless boys, direct intervention by positive male role models can make a difference. Fathers are the best choice, but nearly any man will do in a pinch. God has given men the ability to heal wounded boys just by spending time with them, by caring about them, by investing in them, by sharing their masculine "essence" with them. And usually, men don't even have to do anything special. Often, just letting a boy stand next to him to watch what he does and how he does it spreads spackle into the gap in that boy's soul, healing the tear.

Another area in which fathers and men are especially important is disciplining children. Fathers (or, in your case, grandfathers) have been endowed by God with the mantle of authority within the family. Children have an innate fear of fathers that they don't have of their mothers. Boys who are not disciplined by their fathers do not learn self-discipline, which is a huge factor in male satisfaction in life. Those who are undisciplined are unhappy and grow up to be men who disappoint others in their life.

Boys and young men also need to be tested as part of the maturation process. Those who never test themselves against life never find out what they are made of. They never become confident and secure in their manhood. Trials mature a man in ways that books or lectures never can. If boys are rescued (typically by female mentors) too often growing up, they never learn self-reliance or gain the skills they need to succeed in life. Most often, a boy needs a man to teach him to navigate his way through the brambles and thornbushes of manhood. Without that guidance, too many young boys grow up angry, frustrated, anxious, and scared. Too often they compensate for that by exhibiting a false sense of bravado and self-confidence.

Without the positive behavior modeled by an older male, a boy is left to try to navigate all the difficult circumstances that he will face in life on his own. Boys without fathers are at a huge disadvantage in every area. Many never recover, and so spread destruction and pain wherever they go. Those who do recover struggle with issues their entire lives. Fatherhood wounds are deep, jagged tears in a boy's chest that leave scar tissue in their wake.

Raising your grandchild might be hard—but remember, it's easier to raise healthy children then to fix broken adults.

CHAPTER 7

Healing Abused Kids

Violent homes have the same effect on children's brains as combat on soldiers.

—Daniel Amen, MD

Karen is a grandmother who has fostered more than forty-five teenage girls throughout her life. She told me that *every* girl she fostered had been sexually abused. Every. Single. One. In fact, two of the girls were so severely abused as toddlers by adult men that they suffered from hip dysplasia afterward. It's no wonder that all of these girls each faced significant challenges to leading healthy, happy lives.

Nonetheless, Karen reported that at least a quarter of those girls now have success stories. One, who was adopted from a Russian orphanage at age seven, had to overcome learning disabilities but is now attending college. It just goes to show again that one caring adult can make a difference in a child's life regardless of how much they have been damaged.

Amelia's Story[1]

After many months of play therapy, our granddaughter was finally developing skills to work through her feelings of abandonment. This was great progress for the three-year-old that had only been in our custody for a year! But she was also showing signs of reactive attachment disorder resulting from lack of bonding with her birth mother.

Since her life began in the intensive care unit, withdrawing from her mother's high levels of methadone, I could see how this could happen. Her eyes would not look back at mine when I held her. They almost always closed.

She and I made good progress with our bonding exercises, which we continued practicing at home. She especially liked it when we would take turns feeding each other snacks. Rocking together in a rocking chair didn't hold her interest but swinging together was a hit! I was learning her ADHD brain had its own way of processing. If I could only figure out the key. This became the lifelong challenge in raising our little girl.

Once, our therapist asked how our bonding was going at home. I mentioned a new game our granddaughter had made up, which she wanted me to play over and over again countless times a day. I was so tired of it! The therapist suddenly became very interested in her game.

"She hides, all curled up under her blanket," I explained. "And it is my job to pull the blanket off and exclaim, 'Oh, what a beautiful baby!'"

Our therapist took me and our granddaughter into a room down the hallway, where we would be free from distractions. She handed her a small blanket and asked, "Can you show me your blanket game?"

Our granddaughter happily grabbed the blanket and hid under it on the floor, as usual. I dutifully pulled the blanket off and exclaimed, "Oh what a beautiful baby!" As always, she jumped up, beaming with delight.

The therapist was beaming with delight, too! "Would you like to show my friend your blanket game?" she asked. Our granddaughter happily agreed, and our therapist's supervisor joined us. My grand-daughter and I played the blanket game one more time.

"I have waited a lifetime to see this," the supervisor said as he exited the room.

I later learned that our little girl had created her own version of "rebirthing." It was a controversial therapy that was not commonly practiced, but she had figured it out all on her own. I began to appreciate her creative ADHD brain.

In my book *Healthy Parenting*, I reference facts from "Understanding and Helping Children Who Have Been Traumatized," by Dave Ziegler:

> Our brain consists of billions of individual cells, or neurons, that develop trillions of connections with each other. An infant's brain at birth is only 25 percent developed, allowing it to adapt to many different environments. Therefore, the brain of a child raised by loving parents will develop differently than one raised in a home with a drug-addicted mother and lots of domestic violence. Even if we do not consciously remember these childhood experiences, our brains still do. The brain's primary concern is survival. If survival is threatened, the brain shuts down everything except the self-preservation mechanisms. For a child raised in a violent home where self-preservation is a daily concern, the higher-functioning regions of the brain will become smaller (from lack of use) over time, affecting the child's ability to learn and understand the world,

other than how to survive by being hypervigilant. The good news is, we can change and develop these portions of the brain through plenty of positive reinforcement and nurturing.[2]

Early childhood trauma changes the brain in a several ways. These changes last a lifetime and can lead to adult depression, anxiety, substance abuse, and psychiatric disorders. Many trauma survivors are very resilient but struggle with these day-to-day issues. The DHHS manual, *Foundations Training for Caregivers*, describes trauma in children's brains this way:

> One way that childhood abuse disrupts brain activity is by diminishing its capacity to handle stress. During times of stress, everyone's body releases hormones such as cortisol. This release of cortisol is designed to be brief. However, during times of severe abuse, the brain's ability to turn off that stress response is disabled—keeping the body flooded with cortisol, which causes mood changes, disturbs sleep, heightens anxiety, and causes irritability. This leads to depression, Post-Traumatic Stress Syndrome (PTSD), and other psychiatric disorders, which as an adult will affect the victim's job performance, marriage, parenting, and lead to higher instances of substance abuse.[3]

Children who have been abused internalize profoundly negative messages about themselves and others. These messages persist into adulthood, impacting how they feel about themselves. Perhaps most fundamentally, it hurts their ability to have intimate relationships. Abuse violates the trust at the core of a child's world, limiting his or her ability to have close relationships and leading to chaotic lifestyles.

Even poverty can be a form of abuse in children. A significant percentage of kids being raised by grandparents live in poverty. The American Psychological Association postulates that much like fatherless children, those in poverty are "at greater risk for a number of outcomes including poor academic achievement, school dropout, abuse and neglect, physical health problems, and developmental delays." Psychosocial problems "may include impulsiveness, difficulty getting along with peers, aggression, ADHD, and conduct disorder." They have higher rates of "anxiety, depression, and low self-esteem." Physical health problems include "low birth weight; poor nutrition . . . chronic conditions, such as asthma and pneumonia . . . risky behaviors, like smoking and early sexual activity . . . and exposure to violence." Parents in poverty experience chronic stress, depression, and marital distress, and exhibit harsher parenting behaviors.[4]

Anxiety, PTSD, low self-esteem, depression, chronic pain, interpersonal dysfunction, substance abuse, self-harming behaviors, and suicidal actions are all potential manifestations kids from toxic homes struggle with.

Natalya's Story[5]

Adopted at age thirteen from an orphanage in eastern Europe, Natalya soon left her new parents' home in California with a boy, bound for Mexico. Nearly a year later, she returned home seven months pregnant. After having the baby, it became apparent she could not take care of it. Her adopted grandmother stepped in to care for the little boy for three years while Natalya did drugs and slept around.

The little boy grew up happy and healthy. Finally, after having met someone who appeared to be a stable older man, Natalya asked to have her son back. Two years later, a roommate called Grandma and told her to come and get the boy, as he was being abused. (Natalya and her significant other were staying in a house where drugs and guns were being sold.) After taking custody of the boy once again, Grandma soon observed signs of sexual abuse. He was wildly out of control, inappropriately touched other people's bodies, and had knowledge of sexual practices that no five-year-old should possess. He was later diagnosed with PTSD, OCD, ODD, and ADHD. After years of counseling, great mentoring, and living in a safe, loving environment, he is finally showing signs of healing. He is succeeding in high school and plans to attend college in hopes of working for NASA someday.

It's reasonable to assume that if a child has experienced trauma or abuse, they also suffer from PTSD. Here is how that can affect us and our grandchildren. During times of stress, the adrenal glands produce two chemicals—adrenaline (which causes us to flee) and noradrenaline (which causes us to fight). When we perceive a threat, our bodies instantaneously kick into protective mode. Our brains send a signal to the adrenal glands, and we respond by either fleeing or fighting. A fight response (which is more typical in males) involves things like rage, anger, hyperactivity, impatience, or even abusive behavior. A flight response (generally more typical in females) looks like frustration, isolation, low self-esteem, depression, or suicidal thoughts. Here's the problem: The traumatized brain cannot differentiate between a real threat and an imagined one. So that means if you've had trauma in the past and something today reminds you of that trauma (even things as simple as sounds or smells), it can trigger your brain to order the adrenal glands into action, even if there is no actual threat. The urge to fight or flee can be very strong, and if you don't know what is happening, you'll respond with irrational and inappropriate behaviors as stress hormones flood your body. You'll notice children from traumatic backgrounds often respond to very normal situations irrationally.

Recognizing how children from traumatic environments respond in certain situations and react to various stimuli allows us to understand why they are acting the way they are. This means we can not only have empathy but respond appropriately to their behavior. Additionally, we can help them understand why they feel and act the way they do. This is the first step to correcting negative behaviors.

Healing Wounds

There are several strategies we can use to help heal childhood wounds and trauma. I'll discuss a few below that I've found helpful both personally and professionally. It's important to realize that love, consistent empathy, compassion, and caring, combined with professional counseling, go a long way in helping heal trauma-caused wounds.

Education. In my book *Overcoming Toxic Parenting*, I wrote,

> Betrayal is a huge factor in the wounds received in childhood. When the people on whom we should be able to depend unconditionally for love, shelter, affection, nurturance, and training betray us, it creates jagged wounds that keep us from trusting and even loving others. Wounded children (and adults) tend to exhibit several common characteristics, including holding on to their pain, trying to go it alone, fear of vulnerability, not getting help, resisting change, and never expressing their hurt or anger (understandable if you were punished for expressing those emotions as a child). It takes courage to deal with our pain.[6]

The first step in helping your child heal is to learn about what happened to his brain when he was traumatized. Read books, attend seminars and workshops, and watch videos on the topic. Once you have a basic understanding of what your child is facing, many things that may have seemed confusing suddenly fall into place. Once that happens, you can begin to move forward and help him understand his actions and responses to different stimuli.[7]

Counseling. "Professional help is essential if [a child has] been a victim of physical or sexual abuse."[8] It's important to find a counselor who understands and specializes in childhood trauma. We found tremendous help at a local organization called Morrison Child and Family Services, which provides counseling for traumatized and wounded children. We also got help at The Dougy Center, a free facility dedicated to helping grieving children and families.

Often, play therapy is helpful with younger children. It's important to find the right mental health care professional. They can range from social workers to psychologists or psychiatrists with different levels of education, training, and specialization, and most specialize in different areas of childhood abuse. Not all counselors are right for everyone. In fact, one who is fantastic for one person may not relate well with another. Don't be afraid to keep searching until you find the right one for you and/or your grandchild.

Mentoring. No matter how dysfunctional their homes may have been, with no other examples to judge them against, our grandchildren will assume they were "normal." But most of the people I talk to from abusive or even broken homes who have turned their lives around tell me one very important thing: at some time in their lives they all had a person, couple, or family who modeled for them what a healthy life looked like. It is extremely important to have that vision as a goal to look forward to and to provide hope. As humans, we do not know what we do not know. If we are never exposed to a new "normal," we will continue to think the old version that was modeled for us growing up *is* normal. This can be discouraging and defeating, not to mention destructive to our new family. Also, without that positive role model to replace the negative one, we might eliminate the old one but have only a void in its place. We fill that void with whatever we think is right, which may not work out so well. Without a vision for our future, we always return to our past.

Someone on social media put it this way, "Why do many children in foster care seem so intolerant to a safe, loving home? You know when you run a nice warm bath but you're really cold, and it feels like it's burning your legs so you can't get in? That's how love feels for someone who has never known it."

As grandparents, we can provide an example of a healthy, loving home and family. However, it's important to surround our grandchildren with other examples of healthy people and families. This is easy if you have other family members you are close to. If not, you'll need to find these mentoring situations through friends or acquaintances. Be sure to involve your kids with the families of their friends. (Just be sure to check them out and make certain they are healthy role models!) Kids need to be around other kids their own age. They need that interaction, play, and developmental time. Our challenge was to make sure our granddaughter had plenty of opportunities to play with friends, while also making sure that the friends were not all from backgrounds like hers. She needed to be around healthy, happy, successful people, not just broken ones. We also found our granddaughter needed to be around other adults the age of her biological parents so that she could more easily compare their behavior to that of healthy adults of their generation.

Healing takes place in relationship; we cannot heal alone. When trust has been broken, you can't rebuild it except through another relationship. However, my experience has shown me that broken people tend to take advice from other broken people who reinforce their worldviews, instead of from healthy people who could give them advice that would help. They do this because they feel comfortable around them—they think they "relate" to them. Of course, following their advice is guaranteed to keep them in the same cycle of dysfunction they've lived in their entire lives. Additionally, it's difficult to have healthy relationships with broken people. One of the things you will need to do is literally help your grandchildren "reprogram" their brain and how it functions.

Healing Emotions

In my book *Overcoming Toxic Parenting*, I discuss how feelings (or emotions) "are inherently different from reasoning or knowledge. They arise within us spontaneously rather than consciously. Emotions seem to rule our daily lives. We make decisions based on whether we are happy, angry, sad, bored, or frustrated. We choose activities and hobbies based on the emotions they incite."[9] As psychologists tell us, six basic human emotions experienced across all human cultures are "happiness, sadness, disgust, fear, surprise, and anger."[10]

Perhaps the most important thing we can do for our grand-children is to help them establish trust again. So many abused or neglected children have had their trust shattered by those they depended upon to take care of their basic needs and protect them from harm. This profoundly changes the inner workings of a young child's brain. The only way to heal this wound is for a caring person to intervene in their life and lovingly meet those needs in order to rewire their brains and rebuild trust. Trust, then, is the foundation to healing from all other emotional wounds.

> Emotions are . . . subjective. In other words, anger can encompass a range of levels from mild irritation to blinding rage. Love can range from brotherly friendship to ecstatic adoration. We can feel a variety of emotions all at the same time. We can be both excited and nervous at a job interview, or sad and happy that our child is going off to college. We can even experience conflicting emotions at the same time. It's possible to love and hate a person simultane-ously, or to be both proud of and disappointed in someone. Our emotions are a fundamental part of who we are and how we respond to different situa-tions. [For abuse survivors], those emotional responses are often broken or at least warped.[11]

The good news is that kids are extremely resilient—even those who've been abused. My experience in working with boys

Bob and Sandy's Story[12]

Bob and Sandy took custody of their granddaughter shortly after her second birthday. Her exposure to drug-addicted parents, domestic violence, and neglect prompted them to seek early intervention for potential problems in her development. With an early diagnosis of ADHD, she started play therapy at age three.

She loved the playroom but flitted from toy to toy without focusing on anything. She avoided the dolls but was drawn to the stuffed bugs, snakes, and lizards. Eventually, the therapist directed her to choose a mommy, daddy, and little girl doll to play with. A pattern soon emerged in her play of the "mommy" and "daddy" hitting and yelling at each other. Soon the sad little girl was always looking for "mommy," but "mommy" had disappeared.

Eventually, the therapist taught the grandmother to direct the girl's play at home. At first she wouldn't play with toys. She preferred to be outside running and swinging. But one day Grandma got her to focus on the ladybugs in the hedges. Soon the little girl was catching beetles, crickets, worms, and even baby snakes! Shortly thereafter, she was naming mommies and daddies among the insects, engaging in play therapy on her own. Within days of starting her garden therapy, the mommy and daddy were no longer players in her games. Every critter she chose thereafter was sad because it wanted its mommy.

But today, because of Bob and Sandy's dedication and love, their granddaughter is thriving and healing from her early wounds.

from broken homes is that a loving or caring person can help them heal and prevent them from becoming another statistic.

One way is to help them develop a good attitude. Ensure that they understand they need to be grateful and appreciative for the good things they have in life instead of focusing on all the negatives. We give thanks at every meal for all of our blessings, including good food to eat, a nice home to protect us from the elements, and a loving family to share it with. One thing I've discovered is that no matter how bad our past experiences have been, someone else has always had it worse. Oftentimes focusing on helping those less fortunate than us helps us realize just how lucky we actually are.

Our daughter was very strong-willed growing up. By her teenage years she was a handful. Teenagers are naturally self-focused, but it had gotten to the point where she was making bad and even destructive choices. Toward the end of her junior year of high school I gave her an ultimatum—either switch to the high school where her mother worked and get help, or take her GED and get a job. Frankly, we were fed up with her antics.

One day I heard about a woman who ran a horse ranch that specialized in therapy with special-needs children. In desperation, I took our daughter out there and asked the woman to put her to work. She made her start out by mucking stalls, but soon she was working with the horses and kids. Almost overnight, our daughter's attitude changed.

After that summer, she switched high schools and made the honor roll for the first time. She volunteered to work in PE classes with special-needs students. Her entire demeanor changed all because she was focused on those less fortunate than herself. She spent much of her young adulthood working with special-needs kids, and today she has a career in helping others heal. Sometimes it's all about perspective.

Another emotion that broken kids need to deal with is mourning and grief. I talked about healing *our* grief in Chapter 1; a lot of that information can be applied to your grandchildren as well. Just remember that their grief is probably greater than any you are experiencing, and because they are children, they are unable to process it, articulate it, or even acknowledge it the way you can. That means they need even more compassion, understanding, and professional help than an adult does. The good news, again, is that children are extremely resilient.

Many abused people never grieve or mourn for their loss. One of the challenges of dealing with wounds from childhood abuse is that we have to process our grief. An unfortunate side effect of abuse, however, is that many abused people cannot feel anything—their emotions are frozen. They have had to learn to put their emotions in a box in order to survive. Most abused children are punished for expressing their feelings. So it likely wasn't safe to have feelings in childhood, or they were so painful that they pushed them away in order to cope.

We typically associate grief with the death of a loved one. But in the case of an abusive childhood, the grief is caused by the loss (figurative death) of never having had a loving, nurturing parent-child relationship—the death of childhood innocence. The process of working through grief and starting to feel those emotions again is painful. It takes time and cannot be hurried. There are several stages of grief that we must work through in order to come out the other end.

Grief is a normal response to loss. Grief and anger are often intertwined. It's virtually impossible for one to exist without the other. Children, especially girls, often turn this anger upon themselves, leading to destructive habits or dangerous activities.

Finally, the most powerful healing agent is to help your grandchildren develop a strong faith foundation. "To develop faith is to know hope. Without faith there is no hope. With no hope there is no reason to go on."[13] Having the faith to believe in God's grace and forgiveness lets Him heal our wounds and provide us with hope for the future—the knowledge that even if that past has been ugly, the future is still bright. It's important for kids to remember that their past does not dictate their future unless they allow it to.

CHAPTER 8

Parenting Your Grandchildren

Children need love, especially when they do not deserve it.

—Harold Hulburt

Always remember that your grandchildren still love their mother and father, regardless of what they have or haven't done. Try to not criticize or speak badly of them. That doesn't mean you have to approve or condone their behavior; it just means your grandchildren will find out soon enough (if they don't already know) about their faults without you pointing them out all the time. Then remember to always be there for them when they get disappointed or angry about their parents. Remember also to put your grandchildren's needs ahead of your children's—they are still children, and your kids (their parents) are now adults. That's not always easy, but we need to be aware that it's important.

Additionally, remember that your grandkids already have a mother and father. Even if you are raising them, that may not be

A Parent's Responsibilities

In her book *Toxic Parents: Overcoming Their Hurtful Legacy and Reclaiming Your Life*, Susan Forward writes that:

- A parent must provide for a child's physical needs.
- A parent must protect a child from physical harm.
- A parent must provide for a child's needs for love, attention, and affection.
- A parent must protect a child from emotional harm.
- A parent must provide moral and ethical guidelines for a child.[1]

As I recall, raising my own children wasn't easy, and raising my granddaughter hasn't gotten any easier. It's still kind of fun raising her, but as sassy as she is at eight years old, I'm thinking the teen years are going to be a challenge. This chapter outlines some things to consider when parenting the next generation of children.

your role. If they choose to consider you to be their parents, that's great. If not, be the best grandparent for them you can be.

What Children Need Most

One of the most important things we can do to raise children successfully is to establish nurturing routines. The predictability of a daily routine helps children understand that the world is a safe place where they can learn and grow without fear—and it is something that most kids from abused or neglected backgrounds have lacked. Having a consistent daily routine might include having meals at established times, going to bed at the same time each night (we have a routine of reading, prayers, and tucking in for the night), doing homework at a set time, and daily chores.

Even though she is quite adaptable and flexible, our granddaughter clings to her routine (especially her bedtime routine) like a bear would a honey jar. Any disruption causes a guaranteed commotion bordering on hysteria. She knows she has to do her homework and practice piano after school before she can go play.

Security is imperative for children to feel safe and thrive. Providing it means meeting their needs for shelter, food, clothing, medical care, and protection from harm. Kids need to know they can count on those caring for them. Being dependable and creating a consistent home life is immensely powerful in growing healthy children. Many kids from the foster care system or from abusive situations sneak or hoard food in order to meet this need for security. Be sure they understand that you will always make sure they have enough food and shelter, and that you will provide a safe haven for them.

Stability is also important. Stability consists of a household and extended family that does not have a lot of chaos. Being part of a larger community also ensures a sense of belonging. (Our granddaughter desperately wants extended family in her life—I suppose it is a survival mechanism.) Try to minimize disruptions in your grandchildren's lives if things like divorce, job loss, or illness occur. This isn't always easy under the circumstances, but any stability you can provide helps.

The COVID-19 pandemic and widespread political unrest throughout 2020 disrupted most people's lives. We experienced that as well: Antifa destroyed the downtown area of our city by rioting for 180 straight days, forest fires (presumably intentionally set) raged around the perimeter of our city during the summer months, and family members turned their backs on us due to politics. All were upsetting to the psyche of a young child who couldn't process the sudden changes. All she knew was that adults were troubled by them and she couldn't articulate her fear. In our home, the COVID-19 crisis eliminated (at least temporarily) all of our granddaughter's physical and psychological coping mechanisms, which consisted of playing sports, attending school, drama classes, music lessons, playing with other children, and gymnastics classes. Over time, she started to show regressive behaviors and fell back into old unhealthy habits.

We had to work very hard to provide stability during that time. We did this by continuing as many of her activities as we could—some with other kids and some without. This was even more difficult as we live in the Pacific Northwest, one of the more restrictive areas of the country in terms of social distancing. But we were able to continue her piano lessons, arrange play dates, spend time outdoors (hiking, biking, playing at the park, etc.), and do online counseling sessions. The private school she attends was eventually able to start having in-person classes at least part of the day. My point is that as grandparents of potentially wounded children, we need to recognize how changes affect them and take steps to provide as stable an environment as possible.

The parental care a child receives makes a big difference in the life he or she leads. For instance, just by observing the quality of care a child receives at forty-two months of age, author David Brooks says researchers can predict with 77 percent accuracy whether he or she will drop out of high school.[2]

Make sure your grandchildren get the best possible education for their futures. This includes schooling and also invaluable life lessons from spending quality time with you and other healthy family and friends. People I have spoken to who have overcome abuse and poverty rated education as the most important factor in their success.

Structure is essential for children. Rules, boundaries, and limitations give them a sense of security. Without them, children are forced to grow up too fast and they lose respect for the adults in their lives. Kids without boundaries (even small children) often act out in an effort to find out where those boundaries are.

And of course, what our grandchildren need most is just to be loved—unconditionally if possible, but just loved regardless. Love covers a multitude of mistakes that we make as parents (1 Peter 4:8). Our kids don't expect us to be perfect, but they do expect that we will try our best and not give up.

Healthy Parenting Strategies

All children . . . need clear-cut rules, structure, and guidelines. They thrive under firm supervision and guidance. . . . [Healthy] discipline comes in two forms—internal and external. Internal discipline (or self-discipline) is what we strive to teach our kids by applying external discipline. External discipline is applied in a variety of forms: allowing them to suffer the consequences of their actions, teaching them the pleasures of delayed gratification, understanding the relationship between hard work and success, and through personal accountability. [When children] are not subjected to healthy discipline while growing up, they tend to live unhappy lives and create chaos in the lives of those around them. When we discipline our kids, we are actually preparing them for much more fulfilling lives.[3]

Young people also need to be accountable to someone who will push them to exert the effort required to achieve their best. Coaches are good at this, but other adults such teachers, instructors, and relatives can fulfill that role as well.

Below are several character traits that we need to teach our children for them to grow up healthy and happy:

Self-discipline. All children need to learn to have self-discipline in order to live a contented life. "Self-discipline is the art of controlling one's conduct, feelings, and desires. It is the ability to motivate oneself despite having negative emotions. This requires willpower, restraint, self-control, and persistence. Self-discipline and willpower go hand in hand: Willpower is the strength and

Tips for Teaching Self-Discipline

- Teach children to be grateful—not entitled. Teaching them to say "please" and "thank you" develops gratefulness. Also, giving thanks in prayer models a grateful attitude and helps them develop it.
- Teach them to control their emotions. Teach them the value of focusing on positive emotions like love, hope, and faith instead of being mastered by negative emotions such as jealousy, hatred, and greed.
- Teach them to manage their time effectively. This will benefit them greatly throughout their life. Almost all successful people organize their time well.
- Teach them the benefits of delayed gratification. Our culture promotes instant gratification, which leads to a host of problems including indebtedness, lack of flexibility and choices in life, and not being able to take advantage of opportunities when they become available.

ability to carry out a certain task; self-discipline allows us to use it routinely or even automatically. In other words, if willpower is the muscle, then self-discipline is the structured thought that controls that muscle."[4]

Most people agree that self-discipline is one of the key components to success. Without it, one can never reach their full potential. You could be a naturally gifted musician or athlete, but if you did not have the self-discipline to practice hard and often, you would never reach your full ability. You could be extremely intelligent, but if you did not study and learn, you would waste that ability. We are extremely handicapped if we base our decisions purely on our comfort level. Unfortunately, people today avoid discomfort at all costs. However, if we don't develop the capacity for self-discipline, we deprive ourselves not only of greater chances of success, but larger and long-lasting satisfactions. Undisciplined people are slaves to their appetites, moods, and desires.

So, how do we teach kids to develop self-discipline? One of the keys is to let them experience the consequences (especially negative ones) of their choices. This requires grandparents to not rescue them or bail them out whenever they have a problem. Another way to teach them self-discipline is by disciplining them. Holding them accountable for their actions and meting out appropriate punishment is vital.

Self-discipline requires us to do things we do not want to do. It also requires us to *not* do things we'd like to do. I have to get out of bed and go to work most days. I work from home, so that requires even more self-discipline. I'd prefer to stay in bed all day or go live in a shack on a beach somewhere. But people depend upon me to earn an income so they can eat and have a roof over their heads. The key is to teach our kids to discipline themselves in the things they *need* to do so that they can do the things they *want* to do.

Self-discipline can be taught by doing things as simple as having set bedtimes and wake-up times. Chores like making your bed every morning teach self-discipline. And having consistent dinners each night as a family has proven to benefit many areas of a child's life. As your grandchild gets older, make sure you have a set curfew, and limit the number of nights they can go out each week. Monitor TV and computer time as well.

And of course, like all important things in life, we teach those who look up to us best by modeling behaviors for them. If you want grandchildren who have self-discipline, you must be self-disciplined. If you want them to develop delayed gratification, you have to model that as well. Trust me, you are being watched every minute of every day, and what you do matters.

Compassion. Compassion is the ability to feel sorrow for another's misfortune. It means caring about others and treating them with kindness. It is a shared sense of suffering and the desire to alleviate it. Empathy is the partner of compassion. It is the ability to put yourself in another's shoes, imagining what another is going through. Empathy is the first step to having compassion. Kids who do not learn compassion become self-centered and seldom develop the ability to love others, including themselves.

We can begin to teach our grandchildren about compassion by being compassionate when they are hurt or upset. If you empathize with them, it models what compassion looks like. Empathy is compassion in action.

Discuss compassion in real-life situations. For instance, if a store clerk is rude, you might say to your grandchild, "Wow. That person was really grumpy. She must be having a bad day. What do you think?" That teaches them not to respond to rudeness with meanness.

Help your child learn to recognize facial expressions. Boys especially need this skill, as they typically are less intuitive than girls are. Body language, facial expressions, and tone of voice are all important in helping your grandchild learn to identify and label emotions and what they mean. A fun way to learn this is to watch television with the sound muted and ask them to identify the emotions being expressed.

Pets can be a great way for children to learn about compassion and empathy. Learning to care for a living thing that depends upon them, learning that they have feelings, developing love for them, and experiencing the unconditional love of dogs especially can all teach these valuable traits. And the death of a pet can be a valuable experience for learning compassion. A scene from the movie *Old Yeller* comes to mind: A boy is forced to shoot his dog after he contracts rabies from fighting off a rabid wolf. If you don't cry out of compassion and empathy during that scene, you don't have a heart.

Perseverance. This is the steady persistence or doggedness to overcome obstacles despite difficulties, fatigue, or oppression. It is the ability to work toward a goal without external motivation or reward. It is not quitting even if things seem impossible.

Children (in fact all humans) need to learn perseverance because life is hard. In fact, the things that mean the most in life tend to be the hardest. Anything worth doing is difficult. Persevering through difficult times builds character and faith. It creates success in life.

In his devotional book *90 Days of God's Goodness*, pastor Randy Alcorn says,

> God could create scientists, mathematicians, athletes, and musicians. He doesn't. He creates children who

take on those roles over a long process. We learn to excel by handling failure. Only in cultivating discipline, endurance, and patience do we find satisfaction and reward.[5]

Children who have learned to quit are never able to accomplish anything worthwhile because they do not have the intestinal fortitude to continue when things are tough. They have learned to quit and avoid anything unpleasant like it is the plague. For kids who have experienced the trauma of losing their biological family, this can be especially detrimental.

According to ABC News, "a study published in the *Journal of Early Adolescence* found that dads (and granddads) are in a unique position to instill persistence and hope in their children, particularly in the pre-teen and teen years."[6] Men who model hard work and who keep chipping away at pursuits they care about pass that trait along to their children. Researchers from Brigham Young University found that

> fathers who practiced authoritative parenting, defined as providing feelings of love, granting autonomy and emphasizing accountability to a child—were more likely to have kids who developed . . . persistence, which led to better outcomes in school and lower instances of misbehavior. . . . The study joins a growing body of research that suggests fathers are uniquely important to children's self-regulation and self-esteem.[7]

Not allowing our kids to quit too easily is one way we teach them perseverance. James 1:12 says, "Blessed is the man who perseveres under trial because, having stood the test, that person will receive the crown of life that the Lord has promised to those who love him" (NIV).

I recently heard a politician say during a television interview, "There are only two ways to fail in our country—quit or die." That person knows that perseverance is what separates people who succeed from those who fail. We only truly learn to persevere by being held accountable for the choices and decisions we make. There's no easy way to develop this trait.

Lastly, perseverance requires the ability to accept responsibility for our actions, choices, and decisions. Help your grandchild understand that blaming someone else for their problems is not an effective solution. It only makes them a victim. Of course, that means we must model healthy perseverance and not blame others for *our* problems.

Loyalty. Loyalty is faithfulness to our commitments or obligations. It is "a feeling or attitude of devoted attachment and affection."[8] It is also faithfulness to a person, group, cause, or country.

Loyalty is important, as it means we stick by our spouse and children even when times are difficult. It teaches our children that people are faithful to their vows and to their word.

Doing the right thing for the right reason, even if we fail, is not failure. It is faithfulness. And faithfulness is always rewarded.

Not always in the way or timing that we would like, perhaps, but faithfulness and loyalty are *always* rewarded.

Once again, the best way to teach loyalty is through modeling it. What does loyalty look like on an everyday basis? Do we speak highly of our friends (or our spouse) behind their backs, even when they've done something to make us angry? Or do we comment critically on their weaknesses and foibles? Do we defend our spouse even when they've made a mistake? There's a difference between being supportive and loyal versus enabling someone to engage in destructive behaviors. Can your spouse count on your support during times of trouble even when they are sick, ugly, or struggling with life? If you are divorced, do you still show respect for your ex even if you disagree with his or her perspective or lifestyle? What about the mother or father of your grandchildren? Do you make disparaging or critical comments about them—even if they deserve it?

There is a difference between respecting someone and condoning their actions. Respecting them as a person does not mean you condone their actions. It does mean that, for your grandchild's sake, you do not impugn their character or vent your anger toward that person in ways that are damaging.

Most of all, be loyal to your grandchildren. They have been through a lot already. They deserve to have someone in their corner, even when they mess up. Everyone deserves second chances. Hold them to a high standard but allow them to fail, because that's how people learn. If they know you are loyal and have their back, they will respond in kind. You might just need their loyalty someday.

Work Ethic. This is the principle that hard work is intrinsically virtuous or worthy of reward. Someone with a good work ethic believes there is merit in doing hard work and the feeling of satisfaction or enrichment that comes from accomplishing things, rather than from the reward one does or does not get for it. A person with a strong work ethic is motivated to accomplish tasks for the intrinsic value of the work itself. They take responsibility to ensure that tasks are done right, in the proper order and timing.

Your grandchild needs to know and appreciate the value of hard work. No one succeeds in life without working hard. The earlier he or she learns that, the easier their life will be.

One way to train kids to have a good work ethic is by giving them chores from an early age as part of their role in the family. You might even give them a weekly allowance to teach them how to budget money, but they should do some chores with no compensation just because they are part of the family and the chores need to be done. Chores should be age-appropriate, but don't be afraid to make them a little difficult or challenging. It prepares them for the next level, as well as helps them develop a good sense of self-worth through their accomplishments.

Teach them how to work. They are going to work most of their lives and need to learn the principles of how to go about it. The earlier you teach them the principles that help them succeed at work, the easier their lives will be. As an example, few young people today appear to have been taught how to interact with the public. Almost none of the cashiers or fast-food employees I interact with know how to greet me properly, or even say "Please" or "Thank you" for me giving them my money. Perhaps they don't understand that making my experience enjoyable contributes to their getting a paycheck.

Additionally, we need to teach our grandchildren how the free-market system works. Much of what they learn about business and the economy in school is either political propaganda or just plain wrong. When I owned an engineering firm, I had so many college graduates who worked for me say, "My professor never told me I would have to do this kind of work on the job." To which I would reply, "Well, that's why your professor is teaching instead of operating a business."

When our kids do not understand how the free-market economy works, they struggle to get a job or flourish once they have one, and never learn how to start a business. This lack of understanding limits them in many areas of life.

Respect. Manners teach respect. Politeness never goes out of style. Manners show respect for others, regardless of their status or station in life.

Respect is a two-way street. If we want our grandchildren to respect us (and others), we have to respect them. It earns us the right to speak into their lives. We have to be firm but fair in our decision making. We have to be intentional about monitoring and filtering the volume, tone, and kinds of words we speak to them. If we are abusive, we run the risk of losing their respect.

Once lost, respect is more difficult to get back than it was to earn in the first place. One of the biggest ways I see primary caregivers lose the respect of their charges is by not enforcing consistent boundaries in the children's lives. They give in and allow them to get what they want whenever they have a fit. This is a surefire way to lose the respect of a child.

If you've already lost the respect of your child or grandchild (regardless of their age), you can start by offering a heartfelt apology, followed by asking for their forgiveness. A simple, sincere apology goes a long way toward mending fences. All people, even kids, just want to be heard and understood. An apology shows you care enough to try to maintain a relationship.

CHAPTER 9

Leaving a Spiritual Legacy

Grandchildren are God's way of compensating us for growing old.

—*Mary H. Waldrip*

Kids need their grandparents to teach them spiritual truths. If you don't give your grandchildren a spiritual legacy, most likely no one else will, either. They might never get that part of a healthy education. If they have been removed from the custody of their parents for a legitimate reason, they probably didn't receive it in that home. And they certainly will never receive it from a public school, television, movies, songs on the radio, or video games.

Of course, the best way any child learns about spiritual truth is by observing it in people they love and admire. Our daily walk speaks much louder than anything we might say to them or lecture them about. This message coming from grandparents is even more powerful than when it comes from a pastor, priest, or rabbi. Numerous passages throughout the Bible reinforce that we are the primary teachers of faith to our children and grand-children. This doesn't mean that we put a pulpit in the living room and preach a sermon every night, but it does mean we need to be cognizant of our responsibility and aware of ways to instill spirituality in our grandchildren's lives. Here are some things that might make it easier.

Through Our Daily Actions

Do our daily actions reflect our faith? Do we swear or curse others? (Frankly, I sometimes stumble in this area, especially in the car.) Do we show love and grace to other people? Do others know we are people of faith? Are we faithful to our values? Do we honor God? Do we attend church regularly? Do we tithe? All these actions convey what we believe to those who are watching us.

I have often bought lunch for a hungry or homeless person in restaurants we were visiting. This puzzled my granddaughter, and we had some great discussions about what it means to be a Christian and how our actions are a result of our faith.

Through Prayer

Pray daily. We always pray before each meal, giving thanks to the Lord whether at home or at a restaurant. In addition, we always pray with our granddaughter at night before bedtime. We also pray as a family during difficult times or when making tough decisions. Each night before I go to bed I pray over our granddaughter while she sleeps—for God's blessings and protection for her, and that I will be a good enough father for her.

Pray for and with your grandchildren. Teach them to pray by praying out loud at meals. Let them see you praying to God when important decisions need to be made. Pray over them at bedtime (a very powerful experience). Let them see you pray with your spouse if you have one. (Spouses who regularly pray together only have a 1 percent divorce rate.) Kids need to learn to pray because belief in a loving, all-powerful God can assuage many of life's fears. Teach them the power of prayer. It matters.

I heard a story about prayer from some other grandparents raising their granddaughter. Every night while the little girl was growing up, her grandfather would come in and kneel down next to her bed, place his hand on her shoulder, and pray out loud for God's blessings upon her. This went on until the girl went away to college. One year while she was home visiting, she and her grandma were sitting at the kitchen table talking and sipping tea. Out of the blue, the girl asked, "Grandpa still prays for me every night, doesn't he?"

Her grandmother, somewhat startled said, "Why, yes he does. How on earth did you know?"

The girl said, "I can still see his knee marks in the carpet next to my old bed."

I often wonder about that young woman's life and the decisions she makes in college with that kind of legacy. I suspect she makes good ones, knowing she has a grandfather intervening on her behalf with the Creator of the Universe.

Whenever I share that story with the groups I speak to, I always ask how many people were blessed to have a parent pray for them daily. It averages about one out of every hundred attendees. I then ask the rest how they think their life might have turned out differently if they'd had a parent who prayed for them daily. I think my own life might have been spectacularly different.

Reading Devotionals

Each night before our granddaughter's bedtime, my wife reads chapters from a book she likes and from the Bible to her out loud. This allows time for questions and discussions about stories or events in the Bible.

My wife and I also lead a weekly Bible study group. While our granddaughter is not a part of that, she is aware that we are doing it; she sees us do the devotionals and study material each week, and she hears us discussing those studies and our experiences through the weekly prayer requests.

Devotionals don't have to be some stuffy, boring chore. They can be fun. When our kids were growing up, we used to do devotionals at the kitchen table after dinner every night. We found some books called *Sticky Situations*. For each day of the year, these books described a modern "sticky" situation a kid might find himself in and listed four possible solutions to those situations. Typically, one or two of those options were ridiculous (which our kids always eagerly chose as the answer), one might be right, and one was clearly correct. Each story included a Bible verse to review that was relevant to the situation. It was great fun. Even though our kids fake-groaned each night, they have fond memories of it, and they learned some great scriptures while they were at it.

Incorporate Stories from Your Own Life

Nothing conveys information better than stories. Our granddaughter especially loves hearing inspirational stories from our past. Whenever you talk about the past, include spiritual events as well.

My friend Bill served his country for two years in Vietnam. His grandson, Micah, was always bugging him to tell stories about what it was like during the war. Even though he was reluctant to share his experiences, Bill did occasionally share age-appropriate tidbits about his encounters. Micah's favorite was from a time when Bill was surrounded and pinned down under heavy enemy fire. There was no way he was going to get out of that predicament. As he ran out of ammunition, he prayed desperately for God to help him. Out of nowhere, a huge rainstorm swept through the area, allowing Bill to sneak past the enemy lines. Once he was clear, the rain stopped and the sun came out, allowing Bill to find his way back to camp. Bill told his grandson he never doubted that God had answered his prayers.

One story I shared with my kids was this. On the Friday after the 9/11 terrorist attack against our country, I was scheduled to have lunch with my friend Jim. We were in a medium-sized restaurant that was packed with people. While standing in line to order our food, Jim leaned over and whispered, "Rick, President Bush asked us to pray for the victims of 9/11 today at noon. I want to do that. Do you have any suggestions on how I can let everyone in the restaurant know?"

With all earnestness I stuttered, "Uh, no. Better you than me."

At about five minutes to noon, Jim stood up and said in a loud voice, "Excuse me. I don't want to offend anyone, but President Bush asked us to pray for the victims of 9/11 today at noon. We are going to be doing that at our table and I'd like to invite you to join us." Before Jim stood up, the restaurant had been loud, with people talking, doors opening and closing, and pots and pans rattling. But when he started talking, everyone respectfully stopped chatting; after he sat down everyone ignored him and started talking once again as if nothing had happened. Frankly, it was a little embarrassing.

At about ten seconds to noon, a young mom with a little boy walked up to our table and said, "Can we join you? I think what you are doing is awesome." At that, Jim started praying out loud. He prayed a powerfully eloquent prayer for the victims, their families, and our leaders for about ten minutes. The entire time he was praying it was dead silent in the restaurant. I never heard one person talk, no pots or pans clanging, no doors opening or closing, no sound whatsoever.

When Jim stopped, I opened my eyes and was stunned. Literally every person in the restaurant was standing around our table with heads bowed in prayer, including the cooks and servers. Many had tears in their eyes. It was the most powerful thing I had ever witnessed of the power of God being used through a faithful man. I'm positive not all of those people in the restaurant standing around our table were Christians. What an incredible testament to our faith that it motivates even unbelievers to action.

Share Your Testimony

I think it is important to share with our children and grandchildren how we came to know the Lord. Some of the most impactful stories I have ever heard were people's testimonies. Certainly, it needs to be shared at the right time and place in order to be effective.

My testimony is unique to me, but may not be all that unusual. I was raised in an abusive, alcoholic home. I can distinctly remember as a little boy lying in bed at night, my little brothers and sisters huddled around me in fear, my pillow tightly pulled over my ears, desperately crying to God to make the fighting, screaming, and hitting in the next room stop. I prayed fervently, with all my heart and soul. But God didn't answer those prayers—at least, not then.

Growing up with that background, I was determined to succeed on my own. I didn't trust anyone or think I could count on anybody. I followed in the footsteps that were modeled for me. I grew up an angry young man who abused alcohol and drugs as well and took advantage of as many young women as possible.

After somehow getting the most gorgeous woman on the planet to marry me, I started a long process of change. By the time we had our first child, I decided to stop all activities involving alcohol and drugs. That was not a legacy I wanted to pass on to my children. But I proceeded to throw myself into society's most prevalent legal narcotic—work. I became very successful at a young age by running other people's businesses. I then started my own company, an environmental engineering firm.

It eventually became moderately successful, providing us virtually everything our culture says should make you happy. I had a beautiful, loving wife, great kids, a nice home, cars, and so on. But the more I achieved, the less gratifying it was. I found myself becoming more and more despondent. In fact, I distinctly remember driving down the road one day and thinking, *If I just flicked the steering wheel toward that telephone pole, all this pain, anger, and despair would end.* But that also was not a legacy I wanted to leave for my children.

I knew I had to do something to change my life, so I started looking into a variety of religions, studying them to determine if any of them could help me. Frankly, even though I was not a believer, my wife and I had been taking our kids to church for many years because I felt it was good for them to be exposed to the Christian faith. But no one in any of the churches we attended seemed to know we were there, and none cared when we left.

At that point, in frustration, I decided to research men throughout history that I admired to see what had made them so special. As I read about brilliant men such as Leonardo da Vinci, George Washington, John Adams (nearly all of our country's Founding Fathers, in fact), Abraham Lincoln, and many others throughout the ages, the common thread I discovered was that they were all Christians. I was shocked. I had grown up in a family that considered religion in general a crutch for weak people, and Christians in particular to be a bunch of hypocrites.

In reaction to that discovery, I decided to try to disprove the validity of Christianity by studying the Gospel. I spent the next year studying it from every aspect I could. I looked at it generally from an unemotional, scientific perspective—on an anthropological, archeological, geological, and historical basis. After a year, I knew one thing for certain: I could not disprove the validity of the Gospel. In fact, I was convinced that Jesus Christ was a real man, the Son of God, who walked the earth and died for our sins.

At age forty, I turned my life over to a loving God, who in turn forgave me for my sins. What a profound relief that was! From that day forward, my life has never been the same—a fact to which my wife and children can attest. They saw me as both an unbeliever and as a believer. It was a huge blessing in my life that I was able to baptize my wife and both my children. Recently, I was blessed to baptize my granddaughter as well.

Take Them to Church

As I mentioned previously, our daughter was a very strong-willed child growing up. Especially during her teen years, it was tough to be her parent. As I remember, we spent a great deal of time and effort keeping her safe from the decisions she was making. My wife and I, somewhat tongue-in-cheek, said that our biggest goal was just to get her graduated from high school without getting pregnant. Not that she was promiscuous, but virtually every woman on both sides of her family for generations had been unwed teenage mothers. That is a powerful generational curse to try to break.

Our daughter wasn't particularly interested in church sermons, reading the Bible, or study groups. But she was interested in learning the way of God through serving others. So she readily walked with us at prayer vigils outside abortion clinics, served in soup kitchens, and worked with developmentally disabled children. She also worked in our ministry, whether it was childcare at seminars, working with kids at our single moms' camps, or speaking with me at our Father-Daughter conferences.

No one was more shocked than I was when, years later, she turned out to be a godly young woman who faithfully attended church, read her Bible, and prayed daily. I asked her one day how that happened, because she had fought us tooth and nail about anything to do with religion. She said quite simply, "The best thing you ever did was force me to go to church all those years when I didn't want to go."

While that strategy may not work for everyone (and I don't think it was that simple), it is important that our children and grandchildren see us living out the values of our faith. It lays a bedrock foundation for them to bounce things off of as they get older and are exposed to a variety of worldviews. Additionally, being part of a church family exposes them to other people and families who share your value system. While your kids and grandkids won't always listen to everything you tell them, they often internalize it more easily when someone else shares the same information with them. Plus, being in church hopefully allows them to garner friends from families that have a foundation in faith. I'm not naive enough to think all families that go to church are healthy, but the odds of finding ones who are is greater inside church than outside it. Regardless, fellowship with other believers provides a solid foundation for kids to leap from into life.

Help Them Understand

It is very important in transmitting faith to wounded children to help them understand that God did not cause their plight. He does not harm His children. He has given human beings free will. Faith means nothing if it is coerced. Therefore, people can choose to follow God or choose not to (and accept the consequences). That means people have the freedom to choose to harm others. But even in our darkest times, it doesn't mean God is absent. It's possible that He has protected us from even greater harm that we don't know about. And in the bigger picture (which we cannot see), perhaps their wounds are a vital part of events that we cannot comprehend—such as being able to help someone else. There is much about God we cannot fathom, and that's okay. Faith is believing even when we cannot see, hear, or understand the bigger scheme of things.

These little people have had great injustice done to them. Without faith, hope is powerless—it's just a wish. But if it's true that one of God's attributes is justice and that one day we will all have to account for the lives we've led, then they can have faith and hope that all their wounds (and the sins levied against them) will be redeemed.

Encourage your grandchildren to allow God into their hearts. Have them ask God to forgive their sins and have a relationship with them. The love and forgiveness they will experience will heal the holes in their hearts that nothing else can. It is supernatural healing—it's unexplainable. God loves them and He wants to heal their hearts.

CHAPTER 10

Disciplining Children

*We change our behavior when the pain of staying the
same becomes greater than the pain of changing.
Consequences give us the pain that motivates us to
change.*

—Henry Cloud

As I've stated numerous times throughout this book, all
children need healthy discipline and boundaries to become
healthy, happy, and productive adults. They need consistently
applied limits. However, it's not always easy to get children to
buy into things that are good for them. If your grandchildren
are a handful, one remedy is to involve them in the discipline
process. I wrote extensively about this in my book *10 Things
Great Dads Do*:

> One strategy that works well in modifying children's
> behavior (especially strong-willed children) is to allow
> them to participate in designing their own conse-
> quences. That sounds counterintuitive but works

surprisingly well. While setting up or discussing a family value, get your child's input on what the consequences should be if he or she misbehaves. If you haven't already developed a consequence, you can ask your grandchildren what they think is a fair and reasonable idea. That's not to say you don't determine the final consequence, but this at least helps children buy in to the program. Without that, they feel like they have no control over their circumstances.[1]

All forms of discipline have common components that should be followed:

1. Be consistent and fair. Consistency is important in establishing trust and helping your [children] understand your expectations. If you change the rules all the time, you can't expect [them] to know what they are.
2. Use appropriate consequences for each offense.
3. Present a united front with your spouse.
4. Give more praise than correction. Avoid long lectures.
5. Tailor discipline to fit each child's bent. For instance, I had one child who fell apart whenever I barely raised my voice at her. I had another to whom no amount of physical discipline or grounding made a difference. My wife and I had to find creative ways discipline them without either breaking their spirits or allowing them to become bitter and angry.

6. Know the developmental phases that your children go through at different ages.[2]

Healthy discipline should also have several goals in mind. The first is to build trust between the parent [or grandparent] and the child. Trust is the foundation of all human relationships. . . . Once you discipline your [grandchild], don't hold a grudge. The slate is wiped clean and you are starting over—sort of like how God forgives us when we sin and ask for forgiveness. He doesn't hold it against us but forgets all about it.

The second goal is to build self-esteem in the child. If we punish kids too often, they begin to believe [they are] unworthy and unable to be good. As [the primary caretaker], we need to change the belief behind their behavior, not just their behavior. If our [grandchildren] believe they are not capable of being [good people], it doesn't matter how much we discipline them . . . any change will only be temporary, because their behavior will follow the pattern of their beliefs. Our kids' perception of themselves is the key to their attitude, motivation, and behavior. If they believe themselves capable of something, they will be. If they believe they can't do something, they won't even try. Even though all people have value, those who believe they are worthless tend to act as if they are worthless. . . .

Next is to teach them new behaviors. We don't know what we don't know. A child who has never been exposed to a situation . . . cannot be expected to know how to act or what the boundaries are. The best time to learn things is when we make mistakes. It's also important to understand that we learn in stages—knowledge is accumulative. [We build on the basis of our previous understanding]. So often we have to repeat mistakes in order to learn the entire lesson. . . .

Last, discipline (as opposed to punishment in which they have no control) helps a child gain self-control. It teaches them how to think for themselves and how to act in the future when faced with similar situations. They must learn how to manage and control themselves.[3]

When you are contemplating disciplining a child's behavior, take into consideration a few factors to determine how severe the discipline should be:

- Is this behavior typical or part of normal childhood development? A two-year-old (or a teenager) is going to act like a two-year-old from time to time no matter how good the child normally behaves.
- Does the behavior occur at any specific time or occasion? If a child only starts misbehaving or has a bad

attitude right before dinner, perhaps there are issues like blood sugar levels or other factors involved.

- Consider questions like *Why would a child act this way? Is this typical behavior for other children or specific to your child? Is the behavior dangerous, destructive, or illegal* (certainly any of these three would warrant a stronger response than a minor infraction of family rules)? *What are the long-range consequences of this behavior?* Considering those things might give you an idea of how important it is to intervene.
- Last, stay calm and pick your battles. Not everything is worthy of an all-out war. If you fight all the battles, you will eventually lose the war.[4]

Always remember that consequences should be used for both negative and positive situations (good consequences for positive situations and bad consequences for negative situations). Remember to reward the behaviors you like just as often as you discipline the ones you want to correct.

Always remember to follow through with whatever consequences you set for violations of your family rules. If you don't follow through (every single time), everything you do or say will be ignored. We've all seen the parent who keeps repeating "This is the last time!" or who continues to count to three over and over again. These parents have children who are in control of the relationship.

If you do follow through with consequences, you'll find it usually only takes a couple of times for children to stop testing the limits of their boundaries. This works no matter how old they are. Again, it's never too late to change behaviors (in them or in ourselves). Mostly we want to remember that discipline requires us to use firmness, dignity, and respect when exercising our authority.[5]

One of my favorite authors, Dag Hammarskjold, writes in one of my favorite books, *Markings*, "Your position never gives you the right to command. It only imposes on you the duty of so living your life that others can receive your orders without being humiliated."[6]

You can't force your children to obey you. Well, maybe you can—for a while anyway, while they are little. But eventually they will rebel and disobey you, if for no other reason than they can. Also, children can be compliant on the outside and still be disobedient on the inside. That's one reason why screaming, yelling, threatening, and repeating yourself are such ineffective strategies.

When your children [are grown], you probably won't be around all the time to yell at them and force them to make the right decision. A big-picture vision of raising children is to tell them what you expect from them, what the benefits are if they obey, and what the consequences are if they don't. Then let them choose. Of course, that requires you to be very diligent in making sure you follow through with said consequences (both positive and negative). But the goal is to teach them how to make decisions and to know that each decision has consequences. That's a much better way to approach life successfully—especially when they move out of the house and out from under your protection and guidance.

Some of you may have [grandchildren] who are more challenging than others. They may not be able to learn things easily, may struggle in school, and may generally seem unruly or hyperactive and unable to focus. Before allowing the school (or anyone else) to label them as having attention deficit disorder (ADD) or . . . ADHD, you should consider a few things. First, children develop at differing rates and schedules (boys are usually a few years behind girls until at least adolescence). Additionally, the education format used in public schools is generally not conducive to the way most boys learn best. Boys typically struggle with sitting quietly for long periods of time while being lectured to (I still do, and to my knowledge I don't have ADD). Recesses and PE are being cut back, which especially harms boys, who need that release of pent-up energy.[7]

Diagnosing ADHD with any degree of certainty is difficult—primarily because the symptoms (distractability, impulsivity, and hyperactivity) are consistent with normal behavior in all young children.[8] "The challenge is really this: Is the child exhibiting more of any of those traits than he should be for his age?"[9] In my opinion, since nearly all preschoolers exhibit these symptoms, a child shouldn't be diagnosed before the age of seven. Additionally, ADHD-like symptoms such as distractability or hyperactivity can also be caused by a variety of other conditions including sleep disorders, anxiety, or even cultural differences, say experts.[10]

As I note in my book *Heathy Parenting*:

> Also, if your child has been traumatized (which could be anything from a family divorce to having been physically injured in some way), he or she may suffer from some form of Post-Traumatic Stress Disorder (PTSD). PTSD and ADHD look much the same in educational environments, especially for boys. Yet they are very different issues—one is a physical reaction to a traumatic event and the other is a chemical imbalance. Unfortunately, many children with PTSD are misdiagnosed with ADHD and given a stimulant such as Ritalin, which only exacerbates the problem. PTSD is an anxiety disorder (not a concentration issue) and is treated with anti-anxiety medication, pretty much the exact opposite of a stimulant. You can see how that might cause problems.

I am not saying ADD and ADHD are not legitimate diagnoses in some children, but I think too many children today (especially boys) are medicated for just being boys or being naturally rambunctious.

[Caring grandparents] make sure their [grandchildren] are protected from unnecessary and inaccurate labeling, medical procedures, and medication.[11]

Unhealthy Parenting Styles

Even though we grandparents have already raised our own children, it's possible to fall into some bad habits while raising our grandchildren. Understanding our motivations will give us greater understanding of our behavior and how to change it.

As I wrote in my book *Overcoming Toxic Parenting*, the following are some common unhealthy parenting styles. Be aware of tendencies you may have in any of these areas and seek help to remedy them:

Helicopter parents are those who hover over their children, never allowing them to fail. They micromanage their children's lives—never allowing them to control their own schedules, activities and experiences in education, sports, or other facets of life. This does great damage, as children do not learn the valuable attribute of perseverance. Failing, getting up, and trying again until we succeed is not only the best teacher but also develops healthy self-esteem in children. Children who never fail fail to learn. Not suffering the consequences of failure means they don't learn accountability—a requirement for success in life. These parents have control issues from their own childhoods.

Karaoke parents are those who do not present clear boundaries and parameters for their children. They are more concerned with their children liking them than respecting them. They want to be their children's friend. Consequently, their children fail to develop a sense of security and healthy self-esteem. Kids need parents they can respect and look up to, not be friends with. These parents likely suffer from emotional insecurities.

Dry-cleaner parents don't provide their children with proper mentoring or face-to-face time. They abdicate their parental responsibilities and fail to bond with their children (like dropping their clothes off at the dry cleaners for someone else to handle). These parents are often self-centered, oblivious, or feel inadequate to the task of raising their children.

Volcano parents still have unrealized dreams from their pasts which they are trying to fulfill through their children. We all know about Little League Dad, who tries to relive his glory days though his son. Or Beauty Queen Mom, who tries to recreate a dream she gave up on years ago through her daughter. These parents often have baggage from their past that they have not dealt with. Kids will grow up better if their parents have finished growing up first.

Dropout parents fail to be healthy role models who finish what they start or who don't provide the tools their children need. These parents weren't mature enough to have children in the first place and are not ready for that responsibility. Unfortunately, their children end up being unprepared to launch into the world.

Bullied parents lack the courage and strength to lead strong-willed children. Their children are leaderless, as their personalities are stronger than their parents'. These parents lack the backbone to "choose their battles" and not be subservient to their children.

Groupie parents fail to realize their children need leaders, not servants. They lavish too much time and attention on their children, never denying them anything. This can increase the child's self-esteem to unhealthy levels of entitlement. These parents need to recognize that loving their children means treating them as people, not idols. They need to learn when to say no and help them understand that they are not the center of the universe. Otherwise they run the risk of creating narcissistic children.

Commando parents are focused on attaining compliance and perfection in their children because they feel their own reputations are reflected by the children's performance. Consequently, their kids live in anxiety, frustration, and exhaustion from trying to meet these militant expectations.

Finally, **Survivor parents** are those from abusive backgrounds who can often recreate the dysfunction by going too far toward the opposite end of the spectrum and spoiling or overindulging their children. This is usually done in an attempt to put as much distance as possible between their children and the abuse they suffered at the hands of their own parents. However, abuse lies at both ends of that spectrum.[12]

If you recognize any of those patterns in your parenting style, I encourage you to attend some parenting classes, read books, and find support groups to help you understand what is taking place. The good thing about parenting is that it's never too late to become better at it.

CHAPTER 11

Dealing with Agencies

*Let's raise children who won't have to recover from
their childhoods.*

—*Pam Leo*

G randparents often experience legal difficulties related to
obtaining custody or guardianship, enrolling their grandchildren in school, getting benefits from the state, and accessing
medical care for their grandchildren. They may also have concerns related to custody disputes with other grandparents or with
their grandchildren's parents. All in all, working with agencies
is probably the most difficult and distasteful thing grandparents
raising grandkids have to deal with.

Family relationships can be a source of stress. Grandparents
may feel ambivalent about their grandchild's parents—they may
feel compelled to protect their grandchildren from the parents'
issues while also feeling concerned about the parents' well-being.
They may also find it difficult to set limits with the children's
biological parents. Other adult children and grandchildren

sometimes dislike the amount of attention being given to one part of the family or may be concerned about the impact raising another set of children will have on the grandparents' physical and mental health. And some grandparents find it difficult to relate to their grandchildren because of the generation gap.

Try to maintain a relationship with the parents through this process. Those who voluntarily give up their parental rights because they trust you can make the process much smoother. The AAMFT puts it like this:

> Visits from parents can be upsetting, particularly when they are unpredictable or unstable. Additionally, grandchildren may want to spend more time with their parents, but often have difficulty understanding why their parents cannot be more active in their lives.[1]

Here's a familiar story that I heard from many of the grandparents I interviewed for this book. While the details may differ, the irresponsibility and ungratefulness of the parents and the yo-yoing of the child seem to be fairly typical. The following is just one example among many:

> We came to be raising our granddaughter because two people decided that since they had no home or money, why not have a baby? We did not even know [our daughter-in-law] was pregnant until a friend sent a letter letting me know we were going to be grandparents. We

were hoping our son would not reproduce since he had his own problems. They were living with us while she was pregnant and did not even let us know that she was in labor. We found out our granddaughter was born by seeing pictures of other people holding her. Even though we got a loan and bought a house for them to live in and fixed it up, they both were and still are ungrateful. We first got custody of our granddaughter when she was nine months old because she had a yeast infection that was flaming red. The police were called at 11:30 at night to come get her. They determined she could not stay at the house because of the filth. We had her for five weeks and were told to give her back. Then we got her permanently soon thereafter. But I can't help but believe that the bouncing back and forth between our home and one that was abusive had a traumatic effect on her.[2]

The AAMFT says this about the challenges grandparents may have accessing services:

Grandparents often need a variety of support to manage the demands of raising their grandchildren. However, they may be unaware of the range of services available to their family. Some grandparents also have difficulty accessing available services due to other barriers (e.g., health problems, immigration status, lack of transportation, etc.). Finally, grandparents can experience problems with service providers who are judgmental or treat them disrespectfully.[3]

Several organizations offer resources for grandfamilies. Look for those in places like these:

- grandparenting.org
- grandfamilies.org
- AARP.org
- KEEP (not an acronym) is an evidence-based support and skill-enhancement education program for foster and kinship parents of children aged five through the late teens (KEEP SAFE™). According to the Oregon Social Learning Center, it exists to "support foster families by promoting child well-being and preventing placement breakdowns."[4]
- Alternative high schools, online schools

Additionally, there are several city, county, and state programs available for parenting services and training courses. Most are free or low cost. Keep that in mind and do your homework before you become desperate for help.

The Nature of the Beast

One of the biggest challenges most grandparents raising children find themselves in is dealing with the "system." Many of us are unprepared and uneducated about these agencies and the processes involved. One of the difficulties is that every case can be wildly different depending on the caseworkers, judges, and circumstances. I interviewed several current or former foster care workers from various states. Some worked for their agencies for only a few years, and some had made thirty-year careers of it. The acronyms of their agencies varied, so for ease of reading I'll just refer to them all as working for the Department of Human Services (DHS).

The foster care/adoption system tends to be very invasive. That's one of the reasons even good people who want to help abused children hesitate to get involved—they don't want the state in their business all the time. When that happens, foster parents can become the ones being investigated. Add to that the fact that most abused children come with some form of baggage, and many people do not want to introduce those kinds of stresses into their homes.

We were involved in the "system" for three and a half years before our case was finally settled. Our caseworker openly told us it was the state's policy to try to reconcile the children with the biological parents at all costs. While that sounds noble on the surface, it can create ongoing trauma to children over the course of several years if the parents are abusive, addicted, or neglectful. We were also told that state policy swings from one spectrum to the other depending upon the publicity garnered in high-profile cases or new administrations. So if children removed from good homes have terrible outcomes, the state might have a policy of family reunification at all costs. However, if several children are left too long in abusive homes and die, resulting in bad press, the pendulum might swing the other way, causing children to be removed from good homes needlessly.

I will say that most of the workers we dealt with in the system appeared to be good people who cared about the job they were doing. But I think when you continually see the bad side of life (especially involving children), the nature of the beast is to get burned out and jaded. Additionally, large bureaucratic government agency tends to get draconian over time, riddled with regulations and overbearing controls. This causes a vast amount of turnover among employees. Also, new supervisors tend to clean house and hire "their own" people, again causing employee turnover. This can create a continual influx of new and inexperienced employees.

When we were vetted by the DHS to become foster parents prior to taking custody of our granddaughter, we were rubber-stamped almost immediately. Because I had written twelve books on parenting, marriage, masculinity, relationships, and healing from childhood wounds, I was considered a good candidate. Add to that the fact that my wife had taught special-needs students in a public high school for twenty years, and we were accepted before the ink on our background checks was dry. Even though it was late on a Sunday night when the inspector came to our home, I could hear him on the phone telling his superior to process us through immediately. Given our backgrounds, I believe we were treated with as much respect and consideration as anyone ever has been. Nonetheless, our experience going through the foster care program and adoption process was three and a half years of hell.

There were years of visitation with a parent who was never going to get custody back—three times a week at first, and then tapering down to one. There were monthly home inspections, impromptu visits from caseworkers, court appearances, and office meetings. All these were not only time-consuming and expensive, but stressful and invasive. We were told that the state's main objective was to try to reconcile our granddaughter with her mother regardless of what had happened or how inept the parent might be. Never having been in the system before, we had no idea what to expect or even what was going on half the time.

The one blessing through the entire process was our Court Appointed Special Advocate (CASA) worker. She was genuinely concerned for our granddaughter's welfare and advocated for her well-being at every turn. Even though we eventually had to hire an attorney, without our CASA we would have been lost. It appeared to me that, like most industries, everyone involved in the process (caseworkers, attorneys, judges, etc.) were all so used to going through the motions that they lost sight of the fact that the people and families they deal with every day are human beings. They are scared, wounded, confused, anxious, and frustrated. However, as was noted by one former employee of a state agency, when CASA workers are great, they are *great*. When they are not, they're not. If you do not think your CASA worker is doing a good job, you can request another. But we found ours to be invaluable.

How Things Work

In general, here is how things work within these agencies. Please understand that each state is different, with various rules and regulations. This is just an outline to help you get a general understanding. Additionally, please understand that I am a layman and this is my interpretation of how the system works. I apologize in advance for any mistakes—they are entirely my fault and not due to misinformation from any of the people I interviewed.

Initially, a child gets on the agency's radar by someone reporting potential abuse. This could be a relative, neighbor, or even a passerby. Or it could be made by a mandatory reporter such as a teacher, doctor, or coach. (Mandatory reporters are those whose jobs require them by law to report suspected [not proven] abuse of a child to the police or the appropriate state agency.) If the report is considered to have merit, it will be assigned to an investigator from CPS who will interview the reporter, the family, and the child to determine if abuse occurred and whether the child should be removed from the home for his or her own safety. Parental substance abuse and the ensuing neglect are the leading cause of such reports.

If abuse is confirmed, the situation is assigned an ongoing caseworker by a supervisor. Caseworkers can be people who have worked at their job for many years, or your case could be their first. As a caregiver, you will be required to meet with the caseworker multiple times. He or she will discuss the child's well-being, permanency goals, and any upcoming court hearings, observe the child's relationship with the caregiver(s), and evaluate the home environment. He or she will assess the caregiver's ability to provide adequate care (this can be a very invasive process involving finances, background history, etc.) and identify any support or training needs that person may have. Additionally, he or she will discuss visitation with the parents and any requests the parents may have to participate in normal childhood activities.

Typically, within seventy-two hours a hearing is held to determine if the child should remain in custody or return home. Then at various stages, additional hearings are held. After thirty days (in some states this is a longer time frame), the court may review the details of the case during a fact-finding hearing. After ninety days, a disposition hearing is conducted, during which the court orders the parents to participate in services to reduce threats in their home. They will also address visitation and placement issues.

After six months, the first dependency review hearing will be held. The court may determine it is safe for the child to return home, or that he or she should continue to stay where they are. At twelve months, a permanency hearing takes place which determines what the permanent plan for the child should be. At eighteen months (and every six months after that) a permanency hearing is performed. The court reviews whether the parents have participated in services. If they have not made sufficient progress, the court will sometimes order the state to file a petition to terminate parental rights. If a termination petition is filed, there will be a trial during which evidence is presented from both sides. A judge will then decide whether or not to terminate parental rights.

Again, these are just some of the proceedings you can expect to go through, and you can expect some overlap in the time frames between each stage. Different states may have differing programs. Additionally, your situation may be more or less complicated depending on the circumstances.

Regardless, you *will* have to deal with the system. Understand that it is a process and you have to be willing to go through all those steps. I found it to be an arduous and somewhat frustrating process, but one worth dealing with for my granddaughter's sake.

Things to Know

Beyond foster care, there are several types of permanency options including adoption, third-party custody, and guardianship.

The Adoption and Safe Families Act of 1997 (ASFA) is a federal law which was established to promote the safety, permanence, and adoption of children in foster care. The law limits the amount of time a child may stay in foster care by establishing shorter timelines for determining when she or he must have a plan for permanency. The law states that permanency court hearings must be held for children no later than twelve months after they enter foster care; it also states that termination of parental rights proceedings must begin for any child who has been in the care of a state agency for at least fifteen of the last twenty-two months. Exceptions may be made to this requirement if the child is in the care of a relative, or for other compelling reasons. That said, it often takes longer than those timelines to complete the process. We were told the average case takes about three years.

The employees I interviewed described their agencies as ranging from cumbersome (at best) to corrupt (at worst). Like any bureaucracy, there are good people and not-so-good people working there. Unfortunately, in this situation, the stakes are higher and mistakes or misuses of power are amplified, which can cause destruction in innocent people's lives.

The following are some nuggets of advice from former workers:

First, and perhaps most important, follow the parenting guidelines meted out by the state. Reportedly, grandparents are often conflicted between loyalty to their children or their grandchildren. Whether they feel bad for their children or do not want to believe their children would abuse their grandchildren, they have a tendency to allow access and visitation even when prohibited.

My organization, Better Dads Ministries, works with people to help them break generational cycles. So I found it particularly interesting that some DHS workers alluded to the fact that while kinship foster care and adoption has many advantages, there are also some disadvantages—the foremost of which is the potential for generational cycles, which are behaviors passed down from one generation to the next, to continue. For instance, if the child's parents are addicted to drugs, abusive, or neglectful, there is a chance that the grandparents might be as well. Hence, if the agency shows caution in your situation, there may be understandable reasons why.

Be protective of your space and time—don't let DHS run over you. One person told me, "Workers act like they have all the power, but they don't. They only have as much power as you give them." For example, if a caseworker shows up unannounced and demands access to your home, you do not have to let him or her in (although that might not be the best strategy in the long run). Or if a caseworker insists on visiting at a certain time, you have the right to say it does not work for you and schedule a time that does. You shouldn't develop an adversarial relationship with any of the state workers, but you can have healthy boundaries with them.

Bureaucracies do not care about the little guy. We found the best way to deal with them was to be respectful and polite, and we tried to develop a good relationship with everyone we came in contact with. The social worker's attitude goes a long way in making this situation either pleasant or unbearable. The way they present your case to their supervisor or to the court can change things dramatically. Read your state's regulations and determine what your rights are and how things work. It will benefit you in the long run.

Keep your home clean and tidy—this should go without saying. If a child is removed from a neglectful or abusive situation, the last thing an agency may want to do is put them in a similar circumstance.

Show up at all the state hearings and court proceedings dressed nicely. I always wore a sport coat and slacks to each hearing. Always submit a report on how your grandchild is doing, and be prepared to tell the judge more about it if he or she asks for your input. Be polite and well-spoken. Always try to be positive. This can be difficult, as some of these hearings are gut-wrenching—particularly if there is animosity between the parties or parental rights are being removed. My policy was to always take the high ground and to never burn bridges.

State agencies seem to be more concerned, in my opinion, about the abusive parent's rights than the child's rights (which tend to swing back and force with state legislation). In addition, grandparents do not have many rights. You are not a party to the case, so you have no say most of the time. It's why the parents and the child are given an attorney and you are not. This can be frustrating, since you are the one taking care of the child.

Lastly, find groups or people who have been through the process already and seek them out for advice. (See the previous section on kinship-navigator programs and grandparents groups.) Having someone to talk with about what to expect and how they dealt with it can be very beneficial. And just having someone to commiserate with can make life bearable.

CHAPTER 12

The Importance of
Self-Care

Having children is like living in a frat house:
nobody sleeps, everything's broken, and there's a
lot of throwing up.

—Ray Romano

One of the challenges grandparents talk about is not having any free time. When you first start raising your grandchildren, everyone around you says they'll be happy to help you out. Sadly, all those people disappear quickly once the reality of the situation sinks in, leaving you on your own. The lack of family or support resources does not allow grandparents to go out together on dates (without hiring an expensive babysitter), go on vacation, travel, or enjoy their golden years the way many of their peers do.

Another challenge is other grandchildren not in your care who are in the picture. Trying to make sure they are all treated equally is a challenge. Many grandparents have trouble navigating family dynamics, where one child or grandchild feels like they do not get as much attention or as many presents as the grandchild living with them does. One woman said, "I finally just started to try to treat the other children like grandkids, and the ones I am raising like my daughters. That seemed to solve the problem."

Why is self-care so difficult for most of us? Perhaps because that is the very nature of someone who makes great sacrifices for the sake of others. But the results of not taking care of ourselves are devastating to the entire family.

The Family Caregiver Alliance tells us,

> Family caregivers of any age are less likely than non-caregivers to practice preventative healthcare and self-care. . . . Family caregivers are also at increased risk for . . . depression. Caregiving can be an emotional roller coaster. On the one hand, caring for your family demonstrates love and commitment . . . On the other hand, exhaustion, worry, inadequate resources, and continuous care demands are enormously stressful. Studies show that an estimated 46 percent to 59 percent of caregivers are clinically depressed.[1]

But not practicing self-care eventually creates resentment toward your grandchildren. All that to say, self-care may be the most important, yet least appreciated, aspect of the caregiving world.

The Barriers to Self-Care

The biggest challenges to self-care are personal barriers. These attitudes and beliefs keep us from taking care of ourselves.

The first task to removing those barriers is to understand what they are. For instance, do you think you are being selfish if you put your needs first? Do you have trouble asking for help? Does asking for help make you feel inadequate? By understanding what makes us feel that way, we can better advocate for ourselves, which is better for us and our family.

While parents will tell you how tiring and draining raising children can be (and it is), it is nothing compared to being a generation older and raising young children full-time. The day-to-day strain takes a toll both physically and mentally. That's why finding a break or respite care is so important. We have to find the time to recharge our batteries if we are to be effective. Those who are not fortunate enough to have family step in and help out occasionally are desperate to find someone to watch the kids for an evening or even a weekend. Taking a week-long vacation alone seems like a hopeless dream in those circumstances. Babysitters cost a fortune these days, and finding someone you trust to care for and protect your grandchildren for longer than just a night out is difficult—especially if they have special needs or other challenges.

Once we overcome the barriers to self-care, we need to recognize the areas where we need to take care of ourselves. The first is our physical health.

Your Physical Health

Many grandparents find themselves suffering from any number of health ailments. Because of our age, we are more likely

How Can I Help Myself and My Family?[2]

- *Find a support system.* Joining a support group for grandparents raising grandchildren and meeting other people in similar circumstances can provide sense of community.
- *Access available resources.* There are many support services available to grandparents raising grandchildren. If you don't know about them or how to access them, you can ask professionals such as a caseworker, school counselor, or health care provider.
- *Maintain a positive outlook.* Grandparents who look for the benefits of raising their grandchildren, view challenges in a positive way, and maintain an optimistic outlook on life experience much less stress. Less stress means a better life.
- *Take action.* Grandparents who actively cope with challenges tend to experience less stress. When confronted with challenges, take action to resolve or address the issue. Taking action gives us a sense of control and leads to fewer negative outcomes.
- *Engage in self-care.* Take care of your physical and mental health by getting regular exercise, eating right, and getting plenty of rest. (I know—easier said than done.) This might also mean taking a break from the daily demands of raising your grandchildren. Try asking friends or family members to help take care of your grandchildren, even for a short period of time, so that you can rest and recharge.
- *Establish a schedule.* Schedules are vitally important, even for kids who have not experienced trauma in their lives—but having an established family schedule and routine is especially helpful for those who have experienced unstable or chaotic homes.
- *Learn child disciplinary techniques.* Learn the current recommendations for child discipline. Keep yourself educated on issues related to technology, drugs, sex, school, and other issues that your grandchild can (and likely will) face.
- *Use open communication.* Allow your grandchildren to talk openly about their feelings toward their parents and their family situation. Listen closely to what they have to say. You may not agree, but

that's not the point. They need to have someone they trust to bounce their thoughts and emotions off of. And it goes without saying to not talk negatively about your grandchildren's parents in front of them. Nothing good ever comes from that.

- *Set limits.* You may need to set limits with your grandchildren's parents in order to protect yourself and your grandchildren. This may mean not allowing them to visit at times or limiting when and how long they can visit. You can still express support and concern for your grandchild's parents while remaining clear about your expectations. Granted, this may be difficult, especially if one of the parents is your own child, but it's best for everyone involved.

to suffer from heart problems, arthritis, diabetes, hearing and eyesight loss, and a plethora of other challenges. The National Council on Aging states that "approximately 92 percent of seniors have at least one chronic disease and 77 percent have at least two."[3] According to the U.S. Centers for Disease Control and Prevention, "Chronic diseases such as heart disease, cancer, and diabetes are the leading causes of death and disability in the United States."[4]

Caring for grandchildren adds considerable demand to life. The National Institutes of Health suggests that "the exertion and stress associated with fulfilling these demands will exact a health toll";[5] raising young children is "physically taxing and can involve loss of sleep and exposure to infections"; and that added emotional stress and time pressures can eventually lead to overload.[6] Additionally, these sacrifices can lead many grandparents to feel isolated and resentful.[7] "Caring for grandchildren reduces time for self-care, like exercise and going to the doctor,[8] as well as "engaging in hobbies or socializing."[9] "Caring for a grandchild may strain relationships with a spouse or partner, with the child's parent, or with other children or grandchildren."[10] Also, custodial or coparenting grandparents raising their grandchildren have higher rates of depressive symptoms[11] than nonresidential grandparents.[12]

One way to deal with the negative effects on our physical health is to engage in consistent exercise. Take time to go on frequent walks, bike rides, even swimming. (All of which can be done with kids if you can't find childcare.) As we tend to lose flexibility and agility as we get older, it's also important to engage in stretching or balancing exercises. Because I've lifted weights my entire life, I try to get to the gym at least three times a week. Lifting weights helps keep us from losing vital muscle mass as we get older. It also is good for your cardiovascular system.

Another way to maintain good physical health is to eat properly and get plenty of sleep. Healthy eating involves a low-fat diet with plenty of green vegetables. A balanced diet includes healthy levels of protein, carbohydrates, and fats, along with plenty of fresh fruits and vegetables. Cut back or eliminate fast foods or processed foods. My cardiologist told me that if I wanted to walk my granddaughter down her wedding aisle, I needed to make some changes. I cut back on fast foods and sugars and promptly lost twenty pounds. After eating sugar for more than sixty years, I found quitting that to be more difficult than quitting cigarettes. But the negative effects of processed sugar in the body are well-documented. If these lead to diabetes, numerous health risks occur, including stroke, blindness, high blood pressure, heart disease, nerve damage, and the kind of neuropathy that can force one to amputate appendages.

The truth of the matter is, if we do not take care of ourselves, we get sick and even die. We have a huge responsibility to try to live until our grandchildren are adults. Otherwise, they will suffer another traumatic loss in their lives and end up in the foster care system—something I wouldn't wish on any child.

Dealing with Stress

How we perceive and respond to events is a significant factor in how we adjust to and cope with them. Stress comes not only from our circumstances, but how we perceive them. Do we see the glass as half-full or half-empty? Stress levels can be influenced by many factors, including:

- Whether your caregiving is voluntary. If you feel like you had no choice in the matter, chances are greater you will experience distress and resentment.
- Your relationship with the child's biological parent(s).
- Your coping abilities. How you coped in the past predicts how you will cope now. Identify your coping strengths and build on them.
- Whether support is available.

So, what are some steps we can take to manage stress? First, recognize the warning signs. These might include irritability, sleeplessness, and forgetfulness. I tend to get very irritable when I'm stressed out. My wife's shoulders and neck become very stiff and painful. Once you identify the signs, don't wait until you are overwhelmed to take action.

Next, identify the sources of your stress. I know, I smiled when I first heard that too. I think it goes without saying that we all know the biggest source of stress in our lives, right? Besides the little munchkins under our charge, other sources of stress might include having too much to do, family disagreements, feelings of inadequacy or resentment, finances, and the inability to say no. (My wife struggles with that.)

After that, identify what you can and cannot change or control. Remember, we can only change ourselves, not others. Anytime we try to change things we have no control over, we only increase our sense of frustration. But even small changes can make a big difference.

Lastly, take action to reduce your stress. Taking action gives us a sense of control. Figure out what works for you. I once jokingly told someone my stress reducer was yelling at my family. However, that's not a very productive form of relief, as it only increases stress for everyone else.

Some other stress reducers include taking walks, exercising, gardening, meditating, or having coffee with a friend. I find that getting consistent exercise like going to the gym or riding my bike reduces my stress. Getting enough sleep also helps. My wife finds relief in things like gardening, getting massages, and painting. We both find relief in spending some time alone together, like going to the store or having a date night.

Another way to manage stress is to set goals. Know what you want to accomplish over the next several months, then start taking steps toward those things. For example, if your goal is to feel healthier, you can begin by walking three times a week for ten minutes each time. Prioritize these steps, write them down, and establish daily routines. Then begin to say no to requests that are draining, like hosting holiday meals.

Finally, you can deal with stress by letting other people help you. Like a good business manager, you need to learn to delegate the small tasks and focus your energy on the things that are really important. Unfortunately, a lot of caretakers are strong people who either have a difficult time asking others for help or accepting it when it is offered. We don't want to burden others or admit that we can't handle everything ourselves. Additionally, we often struggle with not having any friends to help out. My wife and I have discovered most of the people our age don't want to spend time with us because they want to do things unencumbered by children. (I don't blame them—I would, too, if I weren't raising a child.) And young people with kids our granddaughter's age don't want to hang around with old people. So, we find ourselves in a bit of a Catch-22 situation. That said, friends and support groups can be a huge factor in helping deal with stress.

One grandmother I interviewed for this book put it this way:

Our granddaughter's entry into school and sports was a glaring reminder that our new family unit was different. The parents of her peers were the ages of our adult children. And who would want to hang out with your parents! My husband and I often felt invisible in these awkward social settings. And to add to the mix our ADHD granddaughter had some quirks that only a few were able to overlook. Our friends became the older parents who had kids later in life and/or had quirky kids themselves. So, I was anxious to respond to an ad in our local newspaper inviting grandparents to a support group meeting twice monthly at our community counseling center. Fast forward ten years, and I am still attending this group as its longest-standing member. I plan to graduate when our granddaughter finishes high school in 2022.[13]

I would challenge you to put together a mental list of all the things other people could help with. Fill it with small, simple items so others won't be overwhelmed. That makes it easier for them to want to help you. For instance, it could include taking your child for a short walk a couple times a week or picking things up from the grocery store for you. Every time my wife and I go to the big box store, we ask our neighbor (who is raising her great-grandchildren) to watch our granddaughter. While there, we pick up and pay for several items our neighbor needs. This gives me and my wife a break and allows us to shop unencumbered, our neighbor gets some much-needed food, and her great-grandchildren get another child to play with, which keeps them out of her hair. It's a win-win situation for all of us.

Your Spiritual Health

How is God involved in all this? Your spiritual health may be even more important than your physical health: when you are spiritually healthy you tend to be emotionally healthy—and that correlates directly to your physical health.

That said, from my perspective, it's very difficult to understand how God works in these situations. I spent sixteen years in full-time ministry before our son passed away. I thought I was close to God, but after our son's death I felt barren and bereft of God's presence. Whether that was actually true or not is up for debate, but it *felt* like He had abandoned me in my time of need. These past four years have been tough.

From my perspective, no one loves or hates God as much as a grieving parent. As I said earlier in this book, when you lose your parents, you're an orphan. When you lose a spouse, you are a widow(er). But when you lose a child, either literally or figuratively . . . well, there's no name for that. It's unnatural.

So how do we endure life's tragedies? After all, none of us gets through life unscathed. Perhaps successfully conquering challenges allows us to toughen up to overcome future trials. For example, I thought two-a-day high school football practices in August were tough. But in hindsight, they prepared me for wrestling practice, which was even tougher. Those experiences taught me what I was capable of doing—which was more than I ever thought possible. They made boot camp so much easier than it would have been had I not succeeded in those environments. Developing the self-discipline, perseverance, and toughness from all those experiences prepared me for life's real difficulties. Losing jobs, failing in business, and the ups and downs of marriage and parenting children take a certain grit and intestinal fortitude that needs to be developed beforehand.

Losing a child to death's black cowl has been the toughest thing I've ever had to endure. Couple that with raising a grandchild, and I've officially hit the proverbial jackpot. But one of the greatest tests we can face is to see if we can bless someone else while we are going through our own storm. Like it or not, both you and your grandchild have been through a tragic situation. It's important for you both to recognize that and find the best ways to deal with it. Having healthy spirituality is one of the best ways to meet this challenge head on.

Maybe men and women face these challenges differently, especially spiritually. I sometimes think life's challenges bring women closer to God but push men farther away. When life beats me down, my response is to come out swinging. My wife's is to get on her knees. But perhaps that's just a spiritual weakness in me.

Reed Farrel Coleman may have described this best in his book *Where it Hurts*:

> "Do you realize, I wonder, that all that rage and fury is aimed in the wrong direction?"
>
> I felt the heat rising beneath my skin, bubbling up to the surface. "What's that supposed to mean?" I slammed my gym bag to the ground.
>
> "That you're not angry at God."

"BS!"

"It's the truth, and what's more, you know it, Gus."

"For chrissakes, Bill, if not God, then who?"

"Your son."

I opened my mouth to speak, but only barely human noises came out.

"Abandonment is a very special kind of hell, and no abandonment hurts so like the death of a child."[14]

One of the things I have been blessed with over the years is a prayer team. This is a group of people who faithfully pray for me and my family on a daily basis. In addition, I can contact them with specific prayer requests as they are needed. I cannot prove that this has been beneficial, but I know in my heart that it is the most important factor to having a good life. If you can, find people who are willing to pray for you consistently.

I've also discovered something else that I have found very helpful over the years. No matter how mature or pious we are, there come times when our spiritual walk feels flat or even absent. I have found the "mechanics of faith" to be indispensable during those times: reading the Bible, praying daily, and attending church consistently. This is most important when we most don't want to do any of those things. I liken it to sports, where we practice doing the same things over and over again. Athletes repeat exercises to the point where most are sick of doing them. But they are training their mind (developing neural pathways) and body (muscle memory) to respond to certain situations without having to think about it. They react instantly. This is important

Types of Help[15]

Experts at the AAMFT tell us there are many types of help available, including:

- *Family Therapy.* Family therapy can help families cope with their feelings about their living situation, resolve problems, and improve the quality of their relationships. Family therapists are specially trained to understand the complicated feelings and relationships grandparents and their grandchildren experience. If you believe that therapy for your family could be beneficial, seek a therapist who has experience working with grandparents raising grandchildren.

- *Support Groups.* Many communities offer support groups for grandparents raising grandchildren, and sometimes there are also groups available for grandchildren. Support groups provide participants with an opportunity to talk about their experiences and feelings in a safe environment. Participants can also gain information about local resources, learn from one another, and meet people dealing with similar issues. Good support groups allow time for personal sharing, maintain a positive outlook, structure sharing time, connect participants with sources of support, and help them set and reach goals. To find a support group near you, visit the websites of the organizations listed under "Resources" or contact a trusted professional in your area. Online support communities are also available, though you will want to carefully assess their quality.

- *Other Services.* Grandparents raising grandchildren may be eligible for a variety of other services and support, including financial assistance, food and nutrition programs, free or low-cost medical care, respite care, and housing assistance, to name a few. To learn more about these types of services, ask a trusted professional such as a caseworker, school counselor, or health care provider for recommendations.

spiritually because when a crisis hits, we are prepared to respond instantly in the best way to deal with it. These three spiritual practices keep us close to God even when we don't feel like we are.

People over fifty-five tend to be the most spiritual age group in the U.S. Having a strong faith helps people of all ages deal with challenges and overcome adversity. Pass your faith on to your grandchildren. It may well be the only opportunity they get to know God.

Mental and Emotional Health

Your mental and emotional health is critical to every aspect of your life. It affects how you think, feel, and act. It helps determine how you handle stress, relate to others, and make choices. It is also one of the key components to successfully helping your

Other Helpful Resources[16]

In addition, many groups offer helpful resources:
- Generations United (www.gu.org): Offers a variety of information and resources for grandparents raising grandchildren.
- Grandfamilies.org (www.grandfamilies.org): Provides legal resources and policy information for grandparents raising grandchildren.
- AARP Grandfamilies Guide (https://www.aarp.org/relationships/friends-family/info-08-2011/grandfamilies-guide-getting-started.html): Offers a comprehensive guide related to seeking services. Includes information about how grandparents can obtain assistance from a variety of professionals and organizations. The website also offers a searchable listing of support groups.
- Karen Wright blog (www.raisingyourgrandchildren.com): Information and community for grandparents raising grandchildren.

grandchildren through their issues and raising them to be healthy and happy. The circumstances you are currently facing are difficult enough without having to contend with the challenges of mental and emotional illness.

So when should we consider seeking professional help? All families are different, but the AAMFT says that in general, you should seek help from a professional if 1) you are unable to manage stress, 2) your stress interferes with your ability to function, or 3) "tension and conflict among family members becomes too difficult to manage. Grandparents should also seek help if their grandchildren's problems become too overwhelming to manage themselves."[17]

Childhood abuse, trauma, or neglect is a major trigger for mental and emotional health issues. One way to determine your and your grandchild's mental health is to monitor some key functions, says the Mental Health Foundation. If you have the "ability to learn, express and manage a range of positive and negative emotions, and form and maintain good relations with others," then you probably have good mental health.[18]

The Mental Health Foundation also provides tips to improve your mental health: Keep active, eat well, keep in touch with friends and family, get enough sleep, ask for help when you need it, consume alcohol responsibly, take breaks, get outside frequently, and do some things you are good at. Finding someone you trust to talk to about your feelings can "help you deal with times when you feel troubled."[19] Also, accepting who you are, rather than wishing you were someone else, is important. And finally, caring for others is an important factor in mental health. It brings us closer to others. Some of us might feel that caring for others introduced mental health challenges to begin with. But, according to experts at the world-renowned Cedars-Sinai Medical Center, caring for others raises hormones in our own bodies that regulate mental health and well-being.[20]

Your Sex Life

Even though you are probably in your golden years, sex is still an important aspect of your life. Though it's not popular to talk about it, most grandparents (at least if they have a spouse or a mate) still engage in sexual activities—just probably not as frequently as they used to. And regardless of what young people think, it's still good.

Ever wonder about how often men struggle with sexual urges and what that is like? In an interview with *Esquire*, actor Steve Coogan said, "There's that famous quote from the guy who said when his libido finally subsided in his old age that he felt like he'd spent sixty years chained to an idiot."[22] That sums it up pretty well. In fact, the older I get, the more my lust is becoming a burden.

Even though the urge is not as powerful, no matter how old men get they never really lose that desire for sex, even if their bodies are weak. In fact, in some ways the longing and urges intensify. I suspect it's due to a combination of things: we know we will never sleep with a beautiful young woman again, and we

Benefits of Sex as You Age

Good sex doesn't have to end with your youth, or even with middle age. The experts at HelpGuide tell us it has a host of benefits for senior citizens,[21] including:

- *Improved mental and physical health.* Sex can burn fat, causing the brain to release endorphins, drastically reducing anxiety.
- *Increased lifespan.* Through its health-improving benefits, a good sex life can add years to your life.
- *Solidify relationships.* Sex is a chance to express the closeness of your deepest relationship.
- *Give refuge.* Sex gives you a chance to escape from the sometimes-harsh realities of the world.

are frustrated by the fact that even if we did, our bodies might not be up to the task. If an older man is lucky (very lucky), he will have a wife who still desires sex and satisfies him at least periodically. If he's unlucky, he will suffer and stew and dream of younger days.

I can't specifically speak to how women regard sex in their golden years, but judging from my wife, they still enjoy it as much as men do. Because of worry or embarrassment about their aging bodies and performance, it may be necessary to try new things. Good communication becomes even more important. Expand your definition of sex—it's not just about intercourse.

Physiological changes to both men and women make having sex a different experience as we get older. Health issues such as arthritis, chronic pain, diabetes, heart disease, stroke, or depression can make it less enjoyable.

Men may get erectile dysfunction (ED) as they get older. Certain blood pressure and pain medication, as well as antidepressants, can cause impotence or affect sexual performance. Every friend I have says, "Thank God for the medications now available that treat ED!"

Women may find changes that affect their sexual ability or enjoyment as well. But vaginal dryness or incontinence are easily treated conditions.

Finding healthy sexual outlets and releases is a part of keeping ourselves emotionally and physically vigorous.

Finding Respite: Taking Care of Yourself and Your Marriage

"Respite care provides short-term relief for primary care-givers."[23] It might be for an afternoon or for several days or weeks. Finding and using respite care is critical to maintaining healthy relationships, as well as your own health and well-being.

Respite care might be as simple as asking friends or family "to watch your loved ones so you can take a break to visit friends, go to the gym, or handle other chores . . . Or respite care can mean finding volunteers or paid carers to provide in-home ser-vices" for longer periods of time, "either occasionally or on a regular basis." Whatever form it takes, it is very important for you to get a break to recharge and refresh yourself.

Several states have programs to find and get respite care. For instance, if your grandchild is in counseling, the Oregon Health Plan provides respite homes which have already been approved by the foster care system to provide care at your counselor's request. Unfortunately, if you are like me, you might find it traumatic to drop your grandchild off and leave him or her with strangers for an extended period of time.

Many organizations and agencies suggest teaming up with other "grandfamilies" to trade off providing childcare for each other. In theory, that would seem to work great. However, our experience is that both we and other grandfamilies are so tired and overwhelmed most of the time that it's difficult to take on additional children. But if you can find some support relief in that arena, I say go for it—especially if children are similar in age. That way, they can actually entertain each other, giving a worn-out grandparent some degree of relief.

All that to say, each state has programs that can provide you respite care if you take the time to track them down. Don't be afraid to advocate for yourself and your needs. You cannot give your grandchild the kind of care and love he or she needs if you yourself are withered, burned out, and emotionally or physically drained.

You're a Hero—Even If You Don't Feel Like One

Grandparents, like heroes, are as necessary to a child's growth as vitamins.

—Joyce Allston

In closing, please recognize that you are truly doing God's work: you are saving the lives of innocent children. At the very least, you have given them a chance at life and hope for the future. You may never get the rewards you deserve on Earth for your sacrifices, but you are engaging in very noble endeavors. I know it is difficult to focus on eternal rewards, but I truly believe God will reward us beyond our wildest dreams for taking care of His little children. The work you are doing is eternal in nature, meaning it has relevance into the future and forever. I believe God rewards that kind of sacrifice.

I recognize that eternal rewards seem nebulous or vague. But focusing on the bigger picture often makes life's difficulties easier to deal with. If you've ever set a long-term goal, one of the best pieces of advice is to focus on the big picture, not the daily grind.

My prayer is that the preceding chapters have helped ease your burdens by giving you practical tools to use on an everyday basis to make life easier and more enjoyable. I hope they have inspired you with hope, that your sacrifices are worth making for the blessings you will receive, both now and eternally. And lastly, I hope you feel that you are not alone. Your life and what you are doing matters more than you can imagine. It's said that your ministry in life may not be what you do, but who you raise. Nothing could be truer in your situation.

Years ago, my wife and I started a program called Standing Tall, through which I was privileged to serve as a teacher and mentor for a dozen young men at a local Bible college who, in turn, had agreed to spend time mentoring fatherless boys. I always told these young seminary students that they might never see the results of their actions during their lifetimes, but every boy whose life they touched—and everyone whose life those boys touched—would be changed because of what these young men did. I believe as God looks at those students, He is beaming with pride. These young men are living lives of honor, and I continue to be proud to be associated with them.

Even to this day, some fifteen years later, I still get correspondence from the moms of the boys those young men mentored. Nearly every boy who was in the program beat the statistics: they are all attending college or married with strong families and good jobs. None of the dozens of boys ended up in prison, addicted, or dead.

The sacrifice these young mentors made for others' benefit with no expectations in return, despite carrying a heavy load of college credits and part-time jobs, is what authentic masculinity is all about. It's what we as grandparents are doing in raising our grandchildren. Without us, their lives might be hopeless and broken, their futures bleak.

As you go through the challenges of raising your grandchildren, God is using you to answer prayers and save children, but understand that you are susceptible to attacks from dark forces as well. With awareness, a strong support network, a healthy spiritual life, and God's help, you are more than equipped to withstand them.

In closing I say, "May God bless you!" I pray for each of you to know the joy that comes from persevering through difficult times and coming out the other side in victory. I wish for God's blessings upon you as you realize how important you are in your grandchildren's lives. Mostly, I hope you experience the joy of pure love between a grandparent and grandchild. Relish that and be well on your journey. Peace upon you and yours.

Acknowledgments

I'd like to thank my longtime agent, Greg Johnson, for believing in me and continuing to seek out publishers for me after I had given up on my writing career. He may know me better than I know myself. At the very least he knew there was one more book in this old war horse.

I'd also like to thank the people at Salem Books and Regnery Publishing. They not only sought me out for this book but gave me free rein to write it the way I wanted. Their support and generosity are gratefully appreciated.

Kudos to Karla Dial for ensuring that all the I's were dotted and T's crossed in this book. That's always the hardest part of writing a book. I'm grateful for her diligent and persistent work.

Notes

Introduction

1. Brandon Gaille, "23 Statistics on Grandparents Raising Grandchildren," Father Matters, https://fathermatters.org/23-statistics-on-grandparents-raising-grandchildren.
2. Ibid.
3. Ibid.
4. Marie C. Gualtieri, "Why Some Grandparents Raising Grandkids Can't Get Government Help," Forbes, June 5, 2019, https://www.forbes.com/sites/nextavenue/2019/06/05/why-some-grandparents-raising-grandkids-cant-get-government-help/?sh=51097b591335.
5. Natasha Pilkauskas, "What's Behind the Dramatic Rise in 3-Generation Households?" The Conversation, November 7, 2018, https://theconversation.com/whats-behind-the-dramatic-rise-in-3-generation-households-104523.

6. R. Dunifon, "The Influence of Grandparents on the Lives of Children and Adolescents," *Child Development Perspective* (2013): 7, 55-60, in S. Md-Yunus, "Development of Well-Being in Children Raised by Grandparents," October 20, 2017, Child Research Net, https://www.childresearch.net/papers/rights/2017_02.html.

7. Gregory C. Smith and Patrick A. Palmieri, "Risk of Psychological Difficulties among Children Raised by Custodial Grandparents," *Psychiatric Services* 58, no. 10 (October 2007), https://ps.psychiatryonline.org/doi/10.1176/ps.2007.58.10.1303?url_ver=Z39.88-2003&rfr_id=ori%3Arid%3Acrossref.org&rfr_dat=cr_pub%3Dpubmed&.

Chapter 1: When Your Life Gets Turned Upside Down

1. Elisabeth Kübler-Ross, "The Stages of Grief," Grief.com, https://grief.com/the-five-stages-of-grief.

2. Elizabeth Kübler-Ross and David Kessler, *On Grief and Grieving* (New York: Scribner, 2014), 13, 15.

3. "Grief Can Have Very Real Physical Symptoms," Pathways, https://pathwayshealth.org/grief-support/grief-can-have-very-real-physical-symptoms.

4. "Lily" (not her real name), interview by Rick Johnson, November 2020.

5. National Family Caregiver Support Program, Administration for Community Living, https://acl.gov/programs/support-caregivers/national-family-caregiver-support-program.

6. "Rhonda" (not her real name), interview by Rick Johnson, December 2020.

Chapter 2: Our New Role

1. "Dave and Judy" (not their real names), interview by Rick Johnson, November 2020.

2. Stephen and Janet Bly, *The Power of a Godly Grandparent* (Kansas City: Beacon Hill Press, 2003), 16.

3. Adapted from Rick Johnson, *Becoming Your Spouse's Better Half: Why Differences Make a Marriage Great* (Grand Rapids: Revell Publishing, 2010), 158.

4. Rick Johnson, "Is There a Difference in Educational Outcomes in Students from Single Parent Homes?" (Master's thesis, Concordia University-Portland, 2009), 31–32.

5. Rick Johnson, *The Power of a Man* (Grand Rapids: Revell Publishing, 2009), 80–81.

6. Rick Johnson, *Becoming the Dad Your Daughter Needs* (Grand Rapids: Revell Publishing, 2014), 9.

7. Ibid., 34.

8. "The Father Absence Crisis," *The Father Factor* (blog), National Fatherhood Initiative, https://learning-center.fatherhood.org/the -father-factor-blog/the-father-absence-crisis-infographic.

9. H. S. Goldstein, "Fathers' Absence and Cognitive Development of 12- to 17-Year-Olds," *Psychological Reports* 51 no. 3 (December 1982): 843–48.

10. Johnson, *Becoming the Dad Your Daughter Needs*, 33.

Chapter 3: Challenges of Raising Children Later in Life

1. Jaia P. Lent, "Grandparents Are Raising the Children of the Opioid Crisis," *Aging Today,* April 9, 2018. The ISSN for *Aging Today* in print is 1067-8379. The title was changed in October 2020 to Generations Today and is now available only electronically.

2. Megan L. Dolbin-MacNab and Bradford D. Stucki, "Grandparents Raising Grandkids," American Association for Marriage and Family Therapy, https://aamft.org /Consumer_Updates/grandparents. aspx?WebsiteKey=8e8c9bd6-0b71-4cd1-a5ab-013b5f855b01.

Chapter 4: Advantages of Raising Children Later in Life

1. A. Billing, K. Ehrle, and K. Kortenkamp, "Children Cared for by Relatives: What Do We Know about Their Well-Being?" *The Urban Institute* Series B, no. B-4 (2012), in S. Md-Yunus, "Development of Well-Being in Children Raised by Grandparents," Child Research Net, October 20, 2017, https://www.childresearch.net /papers/rights/2017_02.html.

2. O. W. Edwards and P. D. Andrew, "School-Age Children Raised by Their Grandparents: Problems and Solutions," *Journal of Instructional Psychology* 33, no. 2 (2006): 113-19, in S. Md-Yunus, "Development of Well-Being in Children Raised by Grandparents," Child Research Net, October 20, 2017, https://www.childresearch.net/papers/rights/2017_02.html.

3. Lisa Esposito, "The Health Benefits of Having (and Being) Grandparents," U.S. News, September 13, 2017, https://health.usnews.com/wellness/articles/2017-09-13/the-health-benefits-of-having-and-being-grandparents.

4. Ibid.

5. The Bronfenbrenner Center for Translational Research, "When Grandparents Raise Their Grandchildren," Psychology Today, September 11, 2017, https://www.psychologytoday.com/us/blog/evidence-based-living/201709/when-grandparents-raise-their-grandchildren#:~:text=.

6. The Nelson Study Bible, New King James Version Bible, Titus 2:4, Commentary, 2067.

7. Wiktionary, s.v. "sophron," last edited September 28, 2019, https://en.wiktionary.org/wiki/sophron.

8. Brett McKay and Kate McKay, "Practical Wisdom: The Master Virtue," Art of Manliness, April 24, 2020, https://www.artofmanliness.com/articles/practical-wisdom/#:~:text=According%20to%20Socrates%20and%20his,he%20would%20naturally%20be%20just.

9. The Nelson Study Bible, New King James Version Bible, Titus 2:4, Commentary, 2067.

10. Ibid.

11. Ibid.

Chapter 5: Outcomes of Kids Raised by Grandparents

1. "Mona" (not her real name), interview by Rick Johnson, December 2020.

2. M. L. Dolbin-MacNab, K. A. Roberto, and J. W. Finney, "Formal Social Support: Promoting Resilience among Grandparents Raising

Grandchildren," in B. Hayslip and G. C. Smith, eds., *Resilient Grandparent Caregivers: A Strengths-based Perspective* (New York: Routledge, 2012), 134–51.

3. Megan L. Dolbin-MacNab and Bradford D. Stucki, "Grandparents Raising Grandkids," American Association for Marriage and FamilyTherapy, https://aamft.org /Consumer_Updates/grandparents. aspx?WebsiteKey=8e8c9bd6-0b71-4cd1-a5ab-013b5f855b01.

4. James Windell, "Children Being Raised by Grandparents Often at Risk," Michigan Psychological Association, August 31, 2020, https:// www.michiganpsychologicalassociation.org/index.php?option=com _dailyplanetblog&view=entry&year=2020&month=08&day=31&id =15:children-being-raised-by-grandparents-often-at-risk.

5. Stine Lehmann, Odd E. Havlik, Toril Havlik, and Einar R. Heiervang, "Mental Disorders in Foster Children: a Study of Prevalence, Comorbidity, and Risk Factors," *Child and Adolescent Psychiatry and Mental Health* 7, no. 3 (November 2013), https:// doi.org/10.1186/1753-2000-7-39.

6. Kristin Turney and Christopher Wilderman, "Mental and Physical Health of Children in Foster Care," *Pediatrics: Official Journal of the American Academy of Pediatrics* 138 (November 2016), https:// pediatrics.aappublications.org/content/138/5/e20161118.

7. Harleena Singh, "What Challenges Grandparents Raising Grandchildren Face," AHA Now, May 25, 2012, https://www.aha-now.com/what-challenges-grandparents-raising-grandchildren-face.

8. Oregon Kinship Navigator, Oregon Grandparents and Relatives Raising Kids Facebook page, December 9, 2020, https://www.facebook.com/groups/568019850594852.

9. "Amy" (not her real name), interview by Rick Johnson, November 2020.

10. Study cited by Kimberly Agresta in Jackie Goldschneider, "Children Reap Emotional, Behavioral Benefits from Grandparents, Says Study," NorthJersey.com, February 2, 2018, https://www.northjersey.com/ story/life/family/2018/02/02/ children-reap-emotional-behavioral-benefits-grandparents-says-study/1082129001.

11. B. J. Hayslip and P. Kaminski, "Grandparents Raising Their Grandchildren: A Review of the Literature and Suggestions for

Practice," *Gerontologist* 45 (2005): 262-69, doi.org/10.1093/geront/45.2.262, in S. Md-Yunus, "Development of Well-Being in Children Raised by Grandparents," Child Research Net, October 20, 2017, https://www.childresearch.net/papers/rights/2017_02.html.

12. S. Md-Yunus, "Development of Well-Being in Children Raised by Grandparents," Child Research Net, October 20, 2017, https://www.childresearch.net/papers/rights/2017_02.html.

13. "Paul" (not his real name), interview by Rick Johnson, November 2020.

14. Heidi Redlich Epstein, "Kinship Care Is Better for Children and Families," American Bar Association, July 1, 2017, https://www.americanbar.org/groups/public_interest/child_law/resources/child_law_practiceonline/child_law_practice/vol-36/july-aug-2017/kinship-care-is-better-for-children-and-families.

Chapter 6: Why Grandfathers Matter

1. U.S. Census Bureau, "Current Population Survey, 2006 Annual Social and Economic (ASEC) Supplement," Census.gov, archived from the original on March 4, 2013, https://www2.census.gov/programs-surveys/cps/techdocs/cpsmar06.pdf.

2. Rick Johnson, "Is There a Difference in Educational Outcomes in Students from Single Parent Homes?" (Master's thesis, ConcordiaUniversity-Portland, 2009), 17.

3. U.S. Census Bureau, "America's Families and Living Arrangements: 2020," Table C3, Current Population Survey, 202ASEC Supplement, Census.gov, last revised October 8, 2021, https://www.census.gov/data/tables/2020/demo/families/cps-2020.html.

4. U.S. Census Bureau, "America's Families and Living Arrangements: 2011," Table C8, Current Population Survey, 2011 ASEC Supplement, Census.gov, last revised October 8, 2021, https://www.census.gov/data/tables/2011/demo/families/cps-2011.html.

5. ASPE Human Services Policy Staff, "Information on Poverty and Income Statistics: ASPE Issue Brief," U.S. Department of Health and

Human Services Office of the Assistant Secretary for Planning and Evaluation, September 11, 2012, http://aspe.hhs.gov/hsp/12 /PovertyAndIncomeEst/ib.shtml.

6. National Center for Health Statistics, "Health, United States, 1993," U.S. DHHS (Hyattsville: Public Health Service, 1994), https:// www.cdc.gov/nchs/data/hus/hus93.pdf.

7. C. Osborne and S. McLanahan, "Partnership Instability and Child Well-Being," *Journal of Marriage and Family* 69 (2007): 1065–83, https://psycnet.apa.org/record/2007-14907-012.

8. Edward Kruk, "Father Absence, Father Deficit, Father Hunger: The Vital Importance of Paternal Presence in Children's Lives," Psychology Today, May 23, 2012, http://www.psychologytoday.com/blog/co -parenting-after-divorce/201205/father-absence-father-deficit-father -hunger.

9. Heather A. Turner, "The Effect of Lifetime Victimization on the Mental Health of Children and Adolescents," *Social Science & Medicine* 62, no. 1 (January 2006): 13–27, https:// pubmed.ncbi.nlm.nih.gov/16002198/.

10. Jay D. Teachman, "The Childhood Living Arrangements of Children and the Characteristics of Their Marriages," *Journal of Family Issues* 25, no. 1 (January 1, 2004): 86–111, https://journals.sagepub.com/doi/ abs/10.1177/0192513X03255346?journalCode=jfia.

11. Victoria Secunda, *Women and Their Fathers: The Sexual and Romantic Impact of the First Man in Your Life* (New York: Delacorte, 1992), 211.

12. Rick Johnson, *Becoming the Dad Your Daughter Needs* (Grand Rapids: Revell Publishing, 2012), 39–40.

13. Angela Thomas, *Do You Think I'm Beautiful? The Question Every Woman Asks* (Nashville: Thomas Nelson, 2003), 52.

14. R. H. Wright and N. A. Cummings, eds., *Destructive Trends in Mental Health: The Well-Intentioned Path to Harm* (New York: Routledge, 2005), APA Psychnet, https:// psycnet.apa.org/record/2005-02409-000.

Chapter 7: Healing Abused Kids

1. "Amelia" (not her real name), interview by Rick Johnson, November 2020.
2. Dave Ziegler, "Understanding and Helping Children Who Have Been Traumatized," excerpts from *Traumatic Experience and the Brain, A Handbook for Understanding and Treating Those Traumatized as Children*, adapted in Rick Johnson, *Healthy Parenting* (Grand Rapids: Revell Publishing, 2016), 73.
3. Gleaned from Dave Ziegler, "Understanding and Helping Children Who Have Been Traumatized," DHHS, in Foundations Training for Caregivers, Session 5—Behavior Modification, 1–3, http://www.wfmt.info/wp-content/uploads/2017/08/Ziegler-Understanding-Helping-Children_Global-Crises-Intervention-Resources.pdf.
4. American Psychological Association, "Effects of Poverty, Hunger, and Homelessness on Children and Youth," December 28, 2009, http://www.apa.org/pi/families/poverty.aspx.
5. "Natalya" (not her real name), interview by Rick Johnson, December 2020.
6. Rick Johnson, *Overcoming Toxic Parenting* (Grand Rapids: Revell Publishing, 2016), 51.
7. Adapted from Johnson, *Overcoming Toxic Parenting*.
8. Johnson, *Overcoming Toxic Parenting*, 78.
9. Ibid., 91.
10. Kendra Cherry, "The Types of Basic Emotions and Their Effect on Human Behavior," Verywell Mind, medically reviewed on April 5, 2021, https://www.verywellmind.com/an-overview-of-the-types-of-emotions-4163976.
11. Johnson, *Overcoming Toxic Parenting*, 92.
12. "Bob and Sandy" (not their real names), interview by Rick Johnson, December 2020.
13. Johnson, *Overcoming Toxic Parenting*, 107.

Chapter 8: Parenting Your Grandchildren

1. Susan Forward with Craig Buck, *Toxic Parents: Overcoming Their Hurtful Legacy and Reclaiming Your Life* (New York: Bantam Books, 1989), 31.
2. David Brooks, *The Social Animal: Hidden Sources of Love, Character, and Achievement* (New York: Random House, 2011), 67.
3. Rick Johnson, *That's My Teenage Son* (Grand Rapids: Revell, 2011), 210.
4. Wikipedia, s.v. "Self-discipline," in s.v. "Discipline," last modified October 12, 2021, https://en.wikipedia.org/wiki/Discipline#Self -discipline.
5. Randy Alcorn, *90 Days of God's Goodness* (Colorado Springs: Multnomah Books, 2011), 198.
6. Mikaela Conley, "Persistence Is Learned from Fathers, Says Study," ABC News, June 14, 2012, http://abcnews.go.com/Health/persistence -learned-fathers-study/story?id=16571927#.T99LTI7lPZF.
7. Ibid.
8. The Free Dictionary by Farlex, s.v. "loyalty," n.d., from the *American Heritage Dictionary of the English Language, 5th ed.*, https://www .thefreedictionary.com/loyalty.

Chapter 10: Disciplining Children

1. Rick Johnson, *10 Things Great Dads Do* (Grand Rapids: Revell Publishing, 2015), 168.
2. Ibid., 166–67.
3. Ibid., 168–70.
4. Ibid., 167.
5. Ibid., 170.
6. Dag Hammarskjold, *Markings*, trans. Leif Sjöberg, Wystan Hugh Aude (New York: Knopf, 1964).
7. Johnson, *10 Things Great Dads Do*, 170–71.
8. Gwen Dewar, "ADHD in Children: Are Millions Being Unnecessarily Medicated?" Parenting Science, last modified March 2013, http:// www.parentingscience.com/ADHD-in-children.html.

9. Rick Johnson, *Healthy Parenting*, 144.
10. Marie C. Gualtieri, "Why Some Grandparents Raising Grandkids Can't Get Government Help," Forbes, June 5, 2019, https://www .forbes.com/sites/nextavenue/2019/06/05/why-some-grandparents -raising-grandkids-cant-get-government-help/?sh=51097b591335.
11. Johnson, *Healthy Parenting*, 145.
12. Johnson, *Overcoming Toxic Parenting*, 125–26.

Chapter 11: Dealing with Agencies

1. Megan L. Dolbin-MacNab and Bradford D. Stucki, "Grandparents Raising Grandkids," American Association for Marriage and FamilyTherapy, https://aamft.org /Consumer_Updates/grandparents. aspx?WebsiteKey=8e8c9bd6-0b71-4cd1-a5ab-013b5f855b01.
2. "Gwen" (not her real name), interview by Rick Johnson, December 2020.
3. Dolbin-MacNab and Stucki, "Grandparents Raising Grandkids."
4. Oregon Social Learning Center, "KEEP: Based on Research Conducted at OSLC," https://www.oslc.org/projects/keep.

Chapter 12: The Importance of Self-Care

1. California Department of Social Services, "Fact Sheet: Taking Care of YOU: Self-Care for Family Caregivers," CA.gov, https://www.cdss.ca .gov/agedblinddisabled/res/VPTC2/4%20Care%20for%20the %20Caregiver/Taking_Care_of_You_SelfCare_for_Family _Caregivers.pdf.
2. Adapted from Megan L. Dolbin-MacNab and Bradford D. Stucki, "GrandparentsRaising Grandkids," American Association for Marriage and Family Therapy, https://aamft.org /Consumer_Updates/ grandparents. aspx?WebsiteKey=8e8c9bd6-0b71-4cd1-a5ab-013b5f855b01.
3. "Healthy Aging Facts," National Council on Aging, January 2017, https://www.ncoa.org/article/get-the-facts-on-healthy-aging.
4. National Center for Chronic Disease Prevention and Health Promotion, "About Chronic Diseases," last reviewed April 28, 2021, CDC, https://www.cdc.gov/chronicdisease/about/index.htm.

5. L. N. Grinstead, S. Leder, S. Jensen, L. Bond, "Review of Research on the Health of Caregiving Grandparents," *Journal of Advanced Nursing* 44, no. 3 (2003): 318–26.

6. M. P. Jendrek, "Grandparents Who Parent Their Grandchildren: Effects on Lifestyle," *Journal of Marriage and Family* 55, no. 3 (1993): 609–21.

7. M. Winkler, E. Fuller-Thomson, D. Miller, D. Driver, "Depression in Grandparents Raising Grandchildren: Results of a National Longitudinal Study," *Archives of Family Medicine* 6, no. 5 (1997): 445–52.

8. K. M. Roe, M. Minkler, F. Saunders, G. E. Thomson, "Health of Grandmothers Raising Children of the Crack Cocaine Epidemic," *Medical Care* 34, no. 11 (1996): 1072–84.

9. R. A. Pruchno, "Raising Grandchildren: The Experiences of Black and White Grandmothers," *The Gerontologist* 39, no. 2 (1999): 209–21.

10. R. G. Sands, R. S. Goldberg-Glen, "Factors Associated with Stress among Grandparents Raising Their Grandchildren," *Family Relations* 49, no. 1 (2000): 97–105.

11. Winkler et al., "Depression in Grandparents," 445–52.

12. Mary Elizabeth Hughes, Linda J. Waite, Tracey A. LaPierre, and Ye Luo, "All in the Family: The Impact of Caring for Grandchildren on Grandparents' Health," *The Journals of Gerontology: Series B, Psychological Sciences and Social Sciences* 62, no. 2 (2007): S108–S119, https://doi.org/10.1093/geronb/62.2.S108.

13. Anonymous, interview by Rick Johnson, November 2020.

14. Reed F. Coleman, *Where it Hurts* (New York: G. P. Putnam's Sons, 2016), 490.

15. Adapted from Megan L. Dolbin-MacNab and Bradford D. Stucki, "Grandparents Raising Grandkids," American Association for Marriage and Family Therapy, https://aamft.org /Consumer_Updates/grandparents.aspx?WebsiteKey=8e8c9bd6-0b71-4cd1-a5ab-013b5f855b01.

16. Ibid.

17. Megan L. Dolbin-MacNab and Bradford D. Stucki, "Grandparents Raising Grandkids," American Association for Marriage and Family Therapy, https://aamft.org /Consumer_Updates/grandparents. aspx?WebsiteKey=8e8c9bd6-ob71-4cd1-a5ab-013b5f855b01.

18. "What Is Good Mental Health?" Mental Health Foundation, https:// www.mentalhealth.org.uk/your-mental-health/about-mental-health/ what-good-mental-health.

19. "How to Look After Your Mental Health," Mental Health Foundation, https://www.mentalhealth.org.uk/publications/ how-to-mental-health.

20. Cedars-Sinai Staff, "The Science of Kindness," Cedars-Sinai Blog, February 13, 2019, https://www.cedars-sinai.org/blog/science-of-kindness.html.

21. Melinda Smith and Jeanne Segal, "Healthy Aging: Better Sex as You Age," HelpGuide, August 2021, https://www.helpguide.org/articles/ alzheimers-dementia-aging/better-sex-as-you-age.htm.

22. Steve Coogan, interviewed by Cal Fussman, "Steve Coogan: What I've Learned," *Esquire*, September 12, 2013, https://www.esquire. com/entertainment/news/a23619/steve-coogan-interview-0114.

23. Melissa Wayne, Monika White, and Lawrence Robinson, "Family Caregiving: Respite Care," HelpGuide, last updated November 2020, helpguide.org/articles/caregiving/respite-care.htm.